IEP Tea

Guide

Council for Exceptional Children

Published by Council for Exceptional Children

Library of Congress Cataloging-in-Publication Data

The Council for Exceptional Children

IEP Team Guide

p. cm.
Includes bibliographical references (p.102).
Stock No. P5274 --T.p. verso.
ISBN 0-86586-319-9 (pbk.)

96-8058
CIP

Copyright 1999 by The Council for Exceptional Children, 1920 Association Drive, Reston, Virginia 20191-1589

Stock No. P5274

Printed in the United States of America

10 9 8 7 6 5 4 3

Contents

Acknowledgments

We would like to acknowledge the following sources of information, which were particularly important in the preparation of this book:

The State of Ohio's *Individualized Education Program (IEP): A Tour Book for the Journey*, from which we adapted much useful material.

Pat Guthrie, Assistant Superintendent for Student Services, Warren County Schools, Kentucky, for the information on students with disabilities and state- and local-level general education assessments in Chapter 9.

Alba Ortiz, Director, Office of Bilingual Education, and Professor, Special Education Department of the University of Texas for the information on cultural and linguistic diversity in Chapter 10.

Special appreciation is extended to the following CEC staff for their vision and energy in shepherding this product to completion: Joseph Ballard, Susan Bergert, Jean Boston, Beth Foley, Susan Johnson, Lynn Malarz, Chris Mason, Jay MacIntire, and Nancy Safer.

The Council for Exceptional Children is grateful to our writer, Katherine Frasier, for attending the Revisioning the IEP planning meeting and synthesizing and integrating the perspectives presented with other information from numerous sources. Her clarity in writing and straightforward presentation will help all IEP team members better understand their roles and responsibilities.

Foreword

The development of this book started with a meeting at The Council for Exceptional Children (CEC) in November of 1997. Teachers, parents, state and local administrative staff, policy analysts, and special education experts of various kinds had been invited to attend. As the meeting began, participants were asked to introduce themselves, and given the changes introduced by IDEA '97, to identify what parts of the IEP process they would like to keep, add, or discard. This is a summary of their answers:

▸ Keep the spirit of individualism, supportive services in the least restrictive environment, family involvement, multidisciplinary approaches, and "the heart in the process."

▸ Add a focus on student aspirations and strengths, student-led processes that give students confidence and focus, ways for the IEP team to become "masters of the process rather than servants of the forms," ways to use technology to make the IEP development process easier, and "an IEP that gives me ideas rather than tells me what I have to do or can't do."

▸ Discard "canned" objectives, an overemphasis on short-term objectives, lack of flexibility in reevaluating students, and the volume of paperwork.

During the 2-day meeting, participants urged that we go beyond a minimalist approach to education. They view education as a life-long experience that goes beyond the classroom and what it takes to pass school tests. They urged us to aim for IEPs that were dynamic, living, and incorporate the whole student and his or her aspirations, strengths, needs, and ideas. They also envisioned an IEP development process with which students are closely involved.

These are the wishes of the meeting participants and not all dreams can become reality. But it seems important, at this time of change, to look further and more ambitiously at what the future could be. This is a time of raised hopes for all students and an opportunity for a major change. It will be a challenging process to meet IDEA '97's new requirements, with more responsibilities handed to people who already have their hands full with other tasks. But we believe that these efforts will pay off and better prepare students for independent, constructive, and satisfying lives.

"Revisioning the IEP"
Meeting Participants
November 10 and 11, 1997
The Council for Exceptional Children
Reston, Virginia

Beth Bader
Executive Director
American Federation of Teachers
Washington, DC

Sarah Blake
Employment and Transition
Representative
Mount Vernon High School
Arlington, Virginia

Karen Fognani-Smaus
Coordinator/Staff Development
Aurora Public Schools
Aurora, Colorado

Carol Kochhar
Past President
CEC's Division on Career Development and
  Transition
Professor
Department of Teacher Education and
  Special Education
George Washington University
Washington, DC

Jonathan McIntire
President
CEC's Council of Administrators of Special
  Education (CASE)
Special Education Coordinator
Burr and Burton Seminary
Manchester, Vermont

Margaret McLaughlin
Instructor for the Study of Exceptional
Children and Youth
University of Maryland at College Park
College Park, Maryland

Lauretta Mays
Special Education Teacher
Burrville Elementary School
District of Columbia Public Schools
Washington, DC

Sydney Morris
Information Specialist
National Association of State Directors of
  Special Education
Alexandria, Virginia

Sue Pratt
Immediate Past Executive Director
Citizens Alliance to Uphold Special
Education (CAUSE)
Lansing, Michigan

Sharon Walsh
Governmental Relations Consultant
CEC's Division for Early Childhood (DEC)
Burke, Virginia

Introduction

We have written this handbook for general and special education teachers who are or will be part of an Individualized Education Program (IEP) planning team. This guide will help you by

- Explaining what federal law requires you to do, including new requirements added in 1997.
- Providing practical advice for carrying out your role as an IEP team member.
- Guiding you through the process of developing and revising an IEP.
- Pointing you in the direction of resources you may want or need to do your job well.

We are providing this guidance because the IEP process, designed to support the education of students with disabilities, can be daunting if you've never been part of it before. And even for veterans, new requirements adopted by the Congress in 1997 will take some time to understand and carry out.

On June 4, 1997, President Clinton signed into law the Individuals with Disabilities Education Act Amendments of 1997, hereafter referred to as IDEA '97. What you will notice as you look at the new requirements of IDEA '97, is that some fundamental assumptions about educating students with disabilities are shifting. Since 1975, when the federal government guaranteed each student with disabilities a free and appropriate public education, parents and educators have struggled to make sure that students have *access* to the services they need to proceed with their education. This has been important, and will continue to be important, but other considerations are also being pushed to the foreground.

Since 1975, federal law has also required that students with disabilities be educated with their nondisabled peers in the general education setting as much as appropriate. Many people have worked hard to make this happen, but still, students with disabilities have too often received their services in settings outside of the general education classroom. In addition, although federal laws have also required that students with disabilities receive the same basic curriculum as other students, many districts have still maintained separate curricula and instructional systems for special education students.

At the same time, parents and teachers have become concerned that too many students with disabilities are participating in a watered-down curriculum, that the expectations for their achievement are too low, and that their overall life outcomes suffer as a result. There are concerns about high dropout and unemployment rates. Some people are asking: To what extent does the *general* education community take responsibility for the achievement of students with disabilities? It is also a reality that special education expenditures are being scrutinized, and in the process, people are asking hard questions about what special education programs have been able to accomplish. What do students with disabilities know and what are they able to do as a result of their special programs? What are the outcomes as these students move out of high school and on to college, jobs, and dreams of independent lives?

These are some of the reasons that IDEA was changed. As of 1997, IDEA requires that general education teachers join IEP teams if a student is, or will be placed, in a general education classroom. Together, general and special educators will look at a student's performance and progress in relationship to the general education curriculum, standards, and assessments. They will be challenged to ask whether the standards being set for this student's achievement are high enough and what accommodations, supports, and services will help the student to work toward the general education standards. They will also continue to figure out when a separate setting is appropriate, or when academic content needs to be modified, but they will need to do this within a rubric of higher expectations.

As a result, roles for general and special educators will be redefined. General educators will become more knowledgeable about special education students and instructional strategies, which will help them to teach the diversity of students in their classrooms. Special educators will increasingly work inside general education classrooms as co-teachers, consultants, and specialists in teaching a range of students with special needs, whether they are special education students or not.

These changes in special education are not taking place in a vacuum. Virtually all states are challenging *all* students to achieve at substantially higher levels. The challenge, and it is a big one, is to create one unified education system of high standards for all students, no matter what their individual circumstances or needs.

For many schools, the changes in IDEA will confirm that they are already moving in the right direction. For others, IDEA will change the way IEP team members perceive their work and goals. We expect that some of these changes will be difficult at first and that some IEP teams will need to shift their focus and learn new skills. We are also expecting that our students will benefit as they are challenged to perform at higher levels *and* receive the support to do so.

What will it take to carry out IDEA's new requirements? Good will and teamwork among many local partners will be crucial. Administrative leadership and support will be essential. Training and orientation will be necessary for teachers and administrators at the district level. We need to take advantage of resources such as technical assistance from the federal government and money from technical grants. The reader can find a complete description of federal special education support programs in CEC's annual publication entitled *Federal Outlook for Exceptional Children*.

CEC's assistance doesn't stop with the publication of this guide. We will be providing updates in *CEC Today*, related articles in our journals, new publications, seminars, and satellite conferences. We will be working closely with the Department of Education and national organizations to help them provide professional development, publications and other materials, and technical assistance. Through keeping in touch with our members, we will track local needs and continue to assist teachers who are IEP team members. We will help you to carry out the new changes in IDEA, which we believe point to the right way to proceed toward our future goals for students. We believe that our schools will be stronger and our students better educated because of this initiative.

As a matter of style we have chosen to alternate male and female pronouns when referring to students in alternating chapters.

Chapter 1
IDEA '97: Revisioning Special and General Education as One System

This chapter has two purposes:

- To explain, in general, how and why the Individuals with Disabilities Education Act (IDEA) was changed in 1997.
- To describe a national movement to improve general education, known as "standards-based reform," that will help you to understand why and how IDEA was changed.

Changes in the Individuals with Disabilities Education Act, 1997

Since 1975, the education of students with disabilities has changed dramatically. Prior to 1975 and The Education for All Handicapped Children Act (which was renamed the Individuals with Disabilities Education Act in 1990), students with disabilities usually had their own separate educational programs if they went to school at all. It was a world more focused on the problems and limitations imposed by disabilities, where expectations were low and services for young people were scarce indeed. As a society, we have come a long way in understanding how to keep students with disabilities into the mainstream and support their learning. The Office of Special Education Programs (OSEP) asserts six fundamental principles in its training module:

- A free appropriate public education.
- Appropriate evaluations.
- An individualized education program.
- The least restrictive environment.
- Parent and student participation in decision making.
- Procedural safeguards.

An enormous amount of work by dedicated people throughout the country followed the passage of The Education for All Handicapped Children Act to assure that its provisions and protections would be carried out. It was a great challenge for parents and local educators to carry out the new requirements and essentially create, from the ground level up, a new system for supporting the education of students with disabilities.

As this was happening, the special education system grew up as a separate and parallel system to the general education system. The management, funding, and requirements of the two systems were different. This seemed, at the time, to be a reasonable way to set things up and assure that a system of supports for students with disabilities was permanently established.

In changing IDEA in 1997, Congress acknowledged the impressive track record of past legislation to support students with disabilities. Prior to the enactment of The Education for All Handicapped Children Act in 1975, about one million students with disabilities were denied an education. Since then (*Senate Report,* IDEA '97)

▸   The number of children with developmental disabilities in state institutions has declined by close to 90%.
▸   The number of young adults with disabilities who are enrolled in post- secondary education has tripled.
▸   The unemployment rate for people with disabilities in their twenties is almost half that of their older counterparts.

But concerns remain about the level of academic achievement of students with disabilities and the proportionately high rate at which they drop out of school. There is also concern that too many students from minority backgrounds or who speak English poorly are inappropriately placed in special education. Further, and perhaps most importantly for the Congress, some educators believe that the IEP process is too often focused on paperwork and procedure — rather than centered around improving the success of students with disabilities in their schooling.

Congress intended to improve IDEA with the following purposes (*Senate Report*, IDEA '97):

▸   Strengthening the role of parents.
▸   Ensuring access of students with disabilities to the general education curriculum and reforms.
▸   Focusing on teaching and learning while reducing unnecessary paperwork requirements.
▸   Assisting educational agencies in addressing the costs of improving special education and related services to students with disabilities.
▸   Giving increased attention to racial, ethnic, and linguistic diversity to prevent inappropriate identification and mislabeling.
▸   Ensuring schools are safe and conducive to learning.
▸   Encouraging parents and educators to work out their differences by using nonadversarial means.

IDEA '97 requires that Individualized Education Programs (IEPs) be more closely tied to the general education curriculum, standards, and assessments. The assumption is that there should be high expectations for all students and that most students can work within the general education curriculum with some accommodations and supports. Students may work at different levels, at different paces, and in different ways, but they should all be working toward similar and challenging goals. The emphasis should also be on services that are delivered *inside* the general education classroom. If that can't work, even with supports and services, then the student receives services in a separate setting. But regardless of the setting, most students with disabilities should be working toward the same goals as students who are not receiving special education services.

The changes made in IDEA in 1997 are intended to bring special education students even more squarely into the mainstream of the general education system. Revisions in the law reflect the fact that special education is increasingly seen not as a separate and special *place* for learning — but as a set of *services and supports* that are individually designed to help students to access the general education program. The question for most students is not *whether* they should work within the regular system, but *how* they can work with the content of the general education curriculum — with what accommodations. For a smaller number of special education students, the question will be how the curriculum needs to be modified in content.

The challenge is to see this as an opportunity to raise aspirations for all students by creating a unified education system that works for all students. In decreasing the separation between the worlds of special and general education, there are really two sets of related questions:

- ▸ How can special education programs help students to meet the challenging education standards, curriculum, and assessments that are now being developed in the general education system?
- ▸ How can the general public education system be tailored and individualized to better serve its diverse learners — whether or not those students have disabilities?

Special and general educators have much to offer one another in finding answers to these questions.

Thus, IDEA '97 holds the following kinds of positive implications (McIntire, 1997a):

- ▸ Through access to the general curriculum, effective instructional practices, and high standards, many special education students will improve their academic performance. This will change people's beliefs about what students with disabilities know and can do.
- ▸ Educators will be encouraged to raise their expectations for the performance of students with disabilities, which means that they will hold students accountable at higher levels.
- ▸ The role and responsibility of general education teachers in the development and implementation of IEPs will increase.
- ▸ Collaboration between general and special educators in planning and carrying out IEPs will increase.

- There will be increased attention to and understanding of what accommodations and adjustments are necessary for special education students to access the general curriculum and participate with other students in state- or district wide assessments.
- General educators, principals, and school systems as a whole will feel an increased responsibility for the achievement of students with disabilities.

It also presents significant challenges (McIntire, 1997a):

- The new requirements will result in tasks that administrators and general and special educators may not know how to perform. They will need on-going and high-quality professional development and to "learn as they go." We hope that this guide will give you a head start on this path!
- The most practical and useful steps to take, processes to follow, and results to aim for will emerge over time.
- Special and general educators are being required to take on new challenges and, as with any change, there will be resistance at times.
- In schools where the relationship between special and general educators is fragile, the tension may worsen before it improves.
- As local IEP teams learn their new responsibilities, the process of developing IEPs will be a little harder and take a little longer at first. With practice, increased understanding, and new tools, this will ease.

Although these challenges are real, they will be addressed over time. In some ways, similar challenges were presented by the original passage of The Education for All Handicapped Children Act in 1975. Educators and parents had to learn what they were required to do, and then they had to learn how to accomplish it. Fortunately, the product was well worth the work.

The Standards-Based Reform Movement

Because of the multiple demands made on principals and other administrators, it is important to consider IEP development within a larger context. Therefore, the second half of this chapter will look briefly at improvements that are being made nationwide in education as a whole. For a more detailed discussion of the standards-based reform movement and students with disabilities, see *The Push and Pull of Standards-Based Reform: How Does It Affect Local School Districts and Students with Disabilities?* (The Center for Policy Research on the Impact of General and Special Education Reform, 1998).

The national movement to improve education is commonly known as "standards-based reform." People generally agree that this movement began with the publication of *A Nation at Risk* in 1983, a report that documented the mediocre performance of students nationwide and warned of the consequences for future job markets and the economy. Many educators were alarmed by this report. Early attempts by states to turn this situation around were "top down" in nature, as states took actions such as lengthening school days, increasing high school graduation requirements, or requiring students to pass a basic skills test for high school graduation. But the results of these "top down" strategies were disappointing (Smith & O'Day, 1990).

In 1990, some new ideas about how to reform education were introduced (Smith & O'Day, 1990). These ideas have been adapted, and in a new form, continue to drive educational improvements today. The new ideas were that educational reform should be

- *Based on a unifying vision and goals.* States should create a common and challenging vision of what schools should be like and what students should know and be able to do.
- *Systemic.* All of a state's education policies need to be revised and changed to support the state's new vision of the education system.
- *Supported by changes in the governance of education.* Clear and appropriate roles should be established for the various levels of the education system. For example, the state's role is to set clear, definable goals of excellence for students and schools, while giving local districts and schools more flexibility in figuring out how the state goals can be met.

Inherent in these ideas is the assumption, backed by research, that virtually *all* students can learn challenging content and complex problem-solving skills if their school is capable of providing a sufficiently challenging curriculum and excellent instruction (Smith & O'Day, 1993). As a matter of fact, these education reformers believed that their new ideas could help erase long-standing gaps in student achievement based on factors such as race and poverty.

At the same time, a combination of events, such as the development of national education goals at the 1989 National Education Summit in Charlottesville, Virginia, began pushing many policymakers towards a system of state standards for education based on high expectations for all students. The business community became involved with this movement, and as this happened, a whole new outlook on education began to emerge.

This new vision, borrowed from corporate America, calls on states to reduce their regulation of the "inputs" of education (such as the number of books in a school library) and to focus instead on the "outputs," especially student performance. The ultimate measure of success in education, people argue, is what students know and what they can do — and not, for example, which classes they take in high school. Are levels of student performance adequate, or even impressive, and will today's high school graduates be able to compete successfully with their peers worldwide? These are deemed the most important kinds of questions that we can ask of our schools.

Thus, the "standards-based reform movement," as it presently exists, is unique in its emphasis on the "outputs" of schooling. The American Federation of Teachers reports that every state except Iowa has adopted common academic standards for students, although these standards vary widely (Gandal, 1997). *A central tenet of this movement is to help **all** students to achieve at higher levels, especially those who are now trailing behind because they are participating in simplified or watered-down educational programs.*

Difficult issues are embedded in the varied nature of state standards for education. For example, state standards differ in their vision of the purpose of schooling. That is, some state standards address strictly academic subject areas (such as literature, history, math, and science). Other states have standards that also pay attention to factors such as a student's readiness to work, as well as qualities such as personal responsibility, independence, physical health, and communication skills.

The nature of state standards has caused some controversy. For example, in 1993, Pennsylvania adopted an "outcomes based" education system to define broadly what students should know and be able to do upon high school graduation. This system was widely mistrusted, partly because some of the outcomes were perceived as vague or focused on personal characteristics of students (instead of sticking more strictly with academics). The state is currently replacing these outcomes with rigorous, measurable academic standards in discrete content areas.

But in other states, the adoption of education standards has gone more smoothly. For example, Missouri adopted 73 *Show Me* standards in 1996 to define what high school graduates should know and be able to do. The state educated the public about the new standards in a number of ways, including printing them on paper place mats that were distributed to restaurants. One recent study found that Missouri school district personnel were aware of the *Show Me* standards and predicted that they would impact local schools, although they reported a "wait and see" attitude as more specific curriculum materials were being prepared by the state (The Center for Policy Research on the Impact of General and Special Education Reform, 1998).

What does all of this mean for students with disabilities? When IDEA '97 was adopted, lawmakers specifically considered the participation of students with disabilities in the standards-based reform movement. This was an important thing to do, particularly since the special education community has not, in many instances, been significantly involved in setting new education standards at the state level. IDEA '97 requires that states

- Establish performance goals for students with disabilities that are consistent, to the maximum extent appropriate, with standards for students without disabilities by July 1, 1998.
- Develop performance indicators to track the progress of students with disabilities toward meeting their performance goals that, at a minimum, address performance on assessments, dropout rates, and graduation rates by July 1, 1998.

- ► Include students with disabilities in state- and district-wide assessments, with accommodations where necessary, effective June 4, 1997.
- ► Develop guidelines for the participation of students with disabilities in alternative assessments if they cannot participate in state- and district-wide assessments (for a discussion about alternative assessments, see Chapter 9).
- ► Develop and begin, no later than July 1, 2000, alternative assessments.
- ► Every 2 years, report to the public on the progress of the state, and students with disabilities in the state, toward meeting performance goals.

In addition, the state department of education must report to the public, with the same frequency and in the same detail as it reports on the assessment of nondisabled students:

- ► How many students with disabilities are taking regular assessments.
- ► How many students with disabilities are taking alternative assessments.
- ► How well students with disabilities are performing on regular assessments (no later than July 1, 1998) and alternative assessments (no later than July 1, 2000), if doing so would be statistically sound and not violate the confidentiality of individual students.

These new federal requirements will obviously impact state and district programs in the future. Questions that have thus far received scant attention, such as how the new state standards for education apply to students with disabilities, will need to be examined much more closely. This should help policymakers to understand how the new state standards apply to the full diversity of students in the public schools.

The state requirements regarding assessment are particularly important because assessments are driving education reform in many states. These assessments are being designed to measure whether schools and students are reaching the new education standards. Depending upon the state, there may be rewards or sanctions for districts and schools whose students score well or poorly on state tests. *Assessments are a way for states to make sure that local districts and schools are striving to achieve the new state standards for education.*

But are special education students being included in these assessments? Too often, the answer is "no, they are not." In fact, as states use test scores to reward or penalize schools, schools feel pressured to exclude from assessments students who, it is perceived, might score lower (for example, special education students).

The National Center for Educational Outcomes (NCEO) has sought to discover how students with disabilities are performing on state and district assessments, and they have found that little information exists. Few states have or obtain data on test scores for students with disabilities (Thurlow, Langenfeld, Nelson, Shin, & Coleman, 1997). In one year, NCEO found that 133 different state tests existed, but states could estimate participation of students with disabilities for only 49 tests, which is about 37% of those tests (Elliot, Erickson, Thurlow, & Shriner, in press). NCEO concluded that students with disabilities are excluded to a significant extent, on a range from full participation to complete exclusion. And even when students with disabilities do take state or district tests, their scores are not always reported or used for accountability purposes.

IDEA's new requirements regarding states, assessments, and students with disabilities means that states and the nation will have a better idea about how students with disabilities are faring at school and how they are doing with regard to the general education curriculum. We will find out whether students with disabilities are making progress in meeting the new education standards. The reporting requirements mean that if large numbers of students in any given state are not taking regular assessments, this will become clear to the public and will have to be justified. Further, alternative assessments will finally be available for students who need them.

There are big changes in the works regarding special education students at the state level. These changes are intended to bring students with disabilities into the mainstream of the standards-based reform movement. Again, it is essential to keep all these factors in mind in order to bring about the intended results for students with disabilities.

Chapter 2
What Is an IEP?

The first chapter began describing "what's new" in federal law regarding the education of students with disabilities. Now, we will step back and start from the beginning by considering what an IEP is and what IEP teams do.

When Congress passed The Education for All Handicapped Children Act in 1975, it required that each student receiving special education services have an Individualized Education Program (better known as an IEP) that

- Sets goals for the student.
- Describes what kind of support services the student will receive.

Developing an IEP is a very personal process, in which each student's strengths and needs are assessed and considered by a team of professionals, the parents, and sometimes the student himself. The process itself is important, as team members combine their differing thoughts, hopes, and perspectives into a single plan. The result is the blueprint for a unique educational program, designed to support just one person. Schools use the IEP to guide their provision of services, and parents use it to track whether a student is receiving services and meeting his goals.

The IEP operates within a unique philosophical context:

- It values all students and respects their differences, supporting their integration into the school and community.
- It looks broadly at the goals of education, beyond high school graduation to establishing a satisfying quality of life and a productive adulthood.
- It acknowledges the primary importance of the family and its participation in every step of the process.
- It emphasizes the role of community as an essential partner with families and schools to help provide services and plan for the transition beyond high school.
- It relies on a decision-making and planning process developed by a team, not by any individual person.
- It strives to intervene early with services to prevent a student's difficulties from evolving into more stubborn and long-term problems.
- It views special education as a set of supportive and individually designed services, not as a place to which a student is assigned.

Thus, the IEP process is a shared responsibility of the community, the family, and the school. The development of an IEP is also part of a *cycle* that begins with a particular student. The cycle has the following steps:

1. *Referral.* The cycle begins when either a parent or teacher notices that the student is struggling with some aspect of his schooling and requests that the student be referred for potential special education services. A committee then meets to decide whether the student's difficulties are severe enough to warrant a formal evaluation. The parents must give permission for the student to be evaluated. In addition, the parents must be invited to this and any other meeting regarding the identification, evaluation, or placement of their student. In this regard, a meeting means a "prearranged event" and not an unscheduled or informal conversation among school personnel.

2. *Evaluation.* Evaluations must be conducted by a multidisciplinary team, and many different methods, tests, and materials are used to evaluate students. The purpose is to understand the student's strengths and needs. The team may look at issues such as educational performance, medical history, social interactions at school and at home, psychological evaluations, and other factors. Any information provided by the parents must be considered by the team.

3. *Eligibility.* Once the data have been gathered, the parents and a team of professionals meet to discuss the results of the evaluation and decide if the student has a disability. Definitions of disabilities, such as hearing impairments, emotional disturbances, and specific learning disabilities, are spelled out in state and federal laws. If the answer is yes, then the committee must decide if the student, because of his disability, needs special education.

4. *Development of the IEP.* If the student is found eligible for special education, then the IEP team is formed and meets to develop the IEP.

5. *Implementation of the IEP.* After the IEP has been developed, the student's special education program and services begin.

6. *Annual review.* The IEP Team reviews the student's IEP at least once a year to discuss whether a student is meeting his goals, to set new goals and objectives, and to revise the educational program and services as necessary.

This cycle has six steps, and the IEP team is usually only involved with steps four, five, and six. In some places, however, the IEP team also determines eligibility. This guide will focus on the times that the IEP team convenes to develop and revise the IEP.

The cycle that we have been describing is an orderly one that is required by law. Federal, state, and local requirements and procedures spell this process out in some detail. The process is designed to assure that students receive the services they need, as well as to provide legal protections for the rights of students with disabilities and their families.

But when working with students and their families, it is important to remember that the process can be intimidating. Consider that as the special education cycle rolls on in its predictable way as ordered by law and regulations, parents are experiencing their own kind of cycle:

- *Awareness* of the difficulties their son or daughter is having at school.
- *Information gathering* about the situation.
- *Acceptance* that there is a problem.
- *Planning*, with the school, for supporting the student.
- And finally, *programming* begins for the student.

(Anderson, Chitwood, & Hayden, 1997)

The cycles that schools must follow and that the parents experience don't always work in harmony, and this can cause distress and conflict. For example, a teacher might observe a student who is struggling with mathematics and refer him for an evaluation before the parent accepts that there is a problem. Conversely, the parent may know that a student is struggling and request immediate services, whereas the school is only beginning to follow its required process, beginning with an evaluation of the student, and this will take time. It can be frustrating when the highly ordered IEP process doesn't correspond to a family's urgent request for special help.

Everyone brings feelings to the IEP process. For example, either a parent or a general education teacher may be frustrated by the unfamiliar terminology of special education. Depending on past experiences, the family may feel more or less comfortable working with and talking openly to school workers. Layered on top of this are feelings, hopes, and fears of the families and the students themselves.

Each IEP team member brings different feelings, perspectives, and thoughts into the process, and mutual trust and respect among the partners is what makes this process work. Each member needs to be treated as an important partner, recognizing that each contributes a different point of view, as well as different kinds of support and services. No one partner can "do it all." No one partner can bear all of the praise, blame, and responsibility for supporting a student's success.

A particular challenge for the IEP team is to reflect a vision of the school and the parents, with and for the student. The team must look at a student's strengths, not just at his struggles, and design a challenging program. Teams need to resist the tendency to focus meetings on student "deficits" and spend all of the time discussing what a student can't do. IDEA '97 emphasizes IEPs that begin with student strengths, parent's concerns, and high expectations. Research and common sense tell us that students can do more and be more than we often have expected.

Additional challenges are posed by IDEA '97. IEP teams are required to intensify their efforts toward designing supports that will allow students to be *involved in* and *progress* in the general education curriculum as appropriate. The team is challenged to consider ways that this can be done within the general education classroom. IEP teams are being asked to question whether their expectations for students are high enough and to find new ways to support students as they work toward meeting higher standards.

A final challenge is to keep a firm focus on the team's ultimate goal: the education and development of the student himself. The IEP team is the "student's team." It can be easy to get lost in the process of developing the IEP and in the relationships among team members. The team needs to pull back and reassess itself from time to time, reminding itself of its ultimate mission.

We hope that all of these challenges don't make the process seem too intimidating! Remember that if you are new to the IEP process, there are people in your school who can help. Ask them now about how they have handled some of the issues that we have mentioned. Another, perhaps simpler, way to look at the IEP process is this: Education is a journey that needs a map. To draw a map, you need to know

- ▸   Who's traveling on this journey?
- ▸   Where is he going?
- ▸   How will he get there?
- ▸   What strengths is the student taking with him that will help him in his travels?
- ▸   What help does the student need to complete this journey?

What Information Must Be Included in the IEP?

The IEP must include the following elements. Don't worry if various terms are unfamiliar, as they are defined and described in the following chapters. Requirements that are new as of 1997 are italicized. IEPs must include

1. A statement of the student's present levels of educational performance, *including the ways in which his disability affects his involvement and progress in the general education curriculum. For preschool students, you would consider whether the disability affects the child's participation in any activities that would be appropriate for him.*

2. A statement of *measurable* annual goals for the student, including *benchmarks* or short-term objectives. *These must help the student to be involved in and progress in the general curriculum, as well as meet other educational needs that result from the student's disability.*

3. A statement of the special education, related services, and supplementary aids and services to be provided to the student. This would include *program modifications or supports for school personnel* that will be provided for the student

   ▸ to advance appropriately toward attaining the annual goals,
   ▸ *to be involved and progress in the general curriculum and to participate in extracurricular and other nonacademic activities,* and
   ▸ to be educated and participate with other students with disabilities and nondisabled students in all of this.

4. An explanation of the extent, if any, to which the student will not participate with nondisabled students in the general education class and in extracurricular and other nonacademic activities.

5. *A description of any modifications in state- or-district-wide assessments of student achievement that are needed in order for the student to participate. If the team determines that the student will not participate in such an assessment (or part of an assessment), a statement of why that assessment is not appropriate for the student and how the student will be assessed.*

6. The projected date for the beginning of the services and modifications, as well as their frequency, location, and duration;

7. *Beginning at age 14, and updated annually, a statement of the transition service needs*, and beginning at age 16 (or younger, if appropriate), a statement of needed transition services. See Chapter 12 for more information about this requirement.

8. A statement of how the student's progress toward his or her annual goals will be measured and *a description of how the parents will be regularly informed (by such means as periodic report cards and at least as often as parents are informed of their nondisabled students' progress) of the student's progress toward the annual goals and the extent to which that progress is sufficient to enable the student to achieve the goals by the end of the year.*

The following are also additions to the IEP as of 1997: In developing each student's IEP, the team must consider the strengths of the student, the concerns of the parents for enhancing the education of their student, and the results of the student's initial or most recent evaluation. The team must also consider certain "special factors," if applicable, including

▸ Strategies, including positive behavioral interventions and supports, for students whose behavior impedes their own learning or other students' learning.
▸ The language needs of students with limited English proficiency, as these needs relate to the student's IEP.
▸ Instruction in Braille and the use of Braille for students who are blind or visually impaired, unless the IEP team determines that such instruction is not appropriate for a student.
▸ Students' communication needs, particularly for students who are deaf or hard of hearing.
▸ The need for assistive technology devices and services.

These special factors are discussed in more detail in Chapter 10.

Also new as of 1997: The IEP team is not required to include information under one component of a student's IEP that is already contained in another section. Although this and other requirements regarding the IEP are new, they represent a natural evolution from the original concept of an IEP.

Chapter 3
The IEP Team Members

In Chapter 2, we began to look at the IEP and IEP team. Now, we will consider the IEP team members more closely. IDEA defines the "IEP team" as a group of people who are responsible for developing, reviewing, and revising the IEP for a student with a disability. By law, these people include

- At least one general education teacher, if the student is (or might be) participating in the general education environment.
- At least one special education teacher or provider.
- A representative of the local educational agency who is knowledgeable about specially designed instruction for students with disabilities, the general curriculum, and the availability of local educational agency resources.
- The parents.
- The student, as appropriate.
- Someone who can interpret the instructional implications of evaluation results, who may be another team member .
- Other people whom the parents or the school have chosen to invite.

When the IEP team meets to plan for a student's transition out of high school or into preschool, there may be other team members (see Chapters 11 and 12).

The general education teacher was added to the list of required team members in IDEA '97.

Collectively, the IEP team members should be knowledgeable about

- The student.
- Available services.
- External and internal sources of assistance.
- The IEP process.

In the rest of this chapter, we will consider these team members one by one, discussing their roles, contributions to the team, and particular challenges.

The General Education Teacher

A student's teacher has always been required to join the IEP team, but this could have been a special or a general education teacher. Up to now, school districts may or may not have been including general educators on the IEP team. Now, a general educator must be included if the student "is or may be participating in the regular education environment."

This change falls in line with other changes in IDEA '97. Without the general education teacher's participation, it would be harder for the IEP team to take on its new responsibilities for looking at a student's progress in the general education curriculum, standards, and assessments.

The general education teacher also brings to the IEP team process a knowledge of

- The general education context.
- How the student with disabilities performs in a general education context.
- How the student interacts with her peers.
- The pace of the class.
- Other students.
- The dynamics of the class.
- Approaches for teaching the class as a whole (in contrast to special education techniques for working with small groups or individual students).

When general education teachers are new to the IEP team, it will help if they understand their specific roles. In addition, general educators who have participated in IEP team meetings before may find that their roles may shift. They may be accustomed to presenting their observations and thoughts about the student to the IEP team, but not to being a vital part of the process from beginning to end.

General education teachers need to know that they are important players. They need to know what they are expected to contribute to the process and what kinds of support they will receive in return — for example, substantive help and support in helping a diverse group of students to learn effectively.

To be part of the IEP team, general educators will need to look at their own beliefs and biases regarding students with disabilities. It is important to own up to biases where they exist, but not let them color one's attitude toward a particular student. To be an effective part of the IEP process, general educators will also need to

- Know how to communicate effectively and work within a team context.
- Know how to observe special education students and record their behaviors objectively in order to help IEP teams track these students' progress.
- Describe a student's performance and behaviors to emphasize the student's strengths. Some general educators will need to learn how to describe a student's progress, weaknesses, and needs in appropriate, positive language. The idea is to

describe the progress the student is making, no matter how small, and to focus on how to get to the next step. For example, "Jim can't add" is vague, derogatory, and doesn't describe what Jim *can* do. "Jim can count up to twenty by ones. We are working on having him count to fifty." is more positive, accurate, and points to the next goal.

▸ Convey to the other IEP team members an acceptance and willingness to actively participate in the IEP process.
▸ Be willing to try new approaches in working with students with special needs.
▸ Be willing to ask for additional assistance when this is needed.

The purpose is to get accurate, reliable data on the student's behavior and progress toward meeting her annual goals. For example, objective observations make careful note of times ("Darren pays close attention first thing in the morning, but tends to become distracted and walk around the room in the hour before lunch."), as well as durations ("Kara can sit for five minutes and listen to a story.").

The IEP has a section in which the general educators can describe any support they need to help a student to attain her goals and participate in the general curriculum. This provides an opportunity for the general education teacher to describe what kind of training or assistance would help in carrying out the IEP.

The Special Educator

Special education teachers have always participated in IEP teams. As of 1997, the special education "slot" on the IEP team can also be filled by a special education service provider, a school psychologist, a physical therapist, or other related services personnel. The special educator who participates in a student's IEP meeting should be the person who is, or will be, responsible for implementing the IEP. If, for example, the student's disability is a speech impairment, the special educator would typically be the speech-language pathologist.

The special educator brings to the IEP team meeting:

▸ Knowledge of the student's learning style.
▸ Previous experience with the student.
▸ Observations of the student interacting with peers in a different context, perhaps, than the general education classroom.
▸ Special education techniques and strategies.
▸ Experience working with students individually or in small groups.
▸ Assessment results and test data.

With the changes in IDEA, special educators will be working more closely with general educators on the IEP to understand how students can better function within the general education curriculum. IDEA's new requirements mean that special educators will need to refine and more often use their skills in areas such as:

- Emphasizing student strengths, not just their "deficits."
- Collaborating effectively with general education colleagues.
- Accurately communicating the areas in which students will need support in order to progress in the general education curriculum.
- Understanding differences between the small group and individual techniques they use, and the "whole class" teaching methods of general education classrooms.
- Understanding the context of the general education curriculum and standards.
- Effectively communicating their knowledge and their techniques for working with students.
- Working within general education classrooms.
- Dealing with resistance to using special education techniques in general education classrooms.
- Gathering knowledge about the student in different contexts than they might usually observe, for example, how the student interacts with peers in the general education classroom, on the playground, and at lunch.

As IDEA '97 reemphasizes the inclusion of students with disabilities in general education classrooms, special educators will find themselves providing services in new settings. This will take some adjustment and may be difficult at times. General and special educators need to reach out for help in understanding how this can work. There are a number of models for team teaching, for example. Teachers can present information together, or they can take turns leading a classroom discussion. In classrooms that do not have a team of general and special educators, the general education teacher may appreciate having a special education teacher take over the class for a time, thereby providing an opportunity to observe the classroom from a different perspective. The class can also be broken down into small groups, with the general and special educators working with different groups of students.

If you are a special educator who will begin working within a general education classroom, you might find it helpful to discuss with the general education teacher what kinds of assistance can be provided, such as:

- Information about special education students who are coming into the general education class.
- Information about any other special education teachers and staff who will be working with the general education teacher.
- Assistance with designing schedules for special instruction that fit in with the general education classroom schedule and plans.
- Assistance with designing instructional strategies to meet the unique needs of individual learners.
- Assistance with tasks such as grading, completing assignments, accommodations, modifications, and assessments.
- Communicating with parents and responding to their concerns.
- Setting up inservice or team meetings on issues that need to be addressed.

There are big changes in store for special educators and general educators alike. Only through a "teaming" of these two fields can the new requirements of IDEA '97 be addressed. This collaboration is meant to benefit students, but it won't necessarily be easy to accomplish quickly.

The Local Education Agency Representative

The local education agency representative (LEA) to the IEP team could be a principal, the principal's designee, or someone from the district office. The LEA representative must be qualified to provide, or supervise the provision of, special education. This person should also have the authority to make decisions about the services the agency can provide, commit agency resources, and make sure that any needed services are provided.

IDEA '97 requires that the LEA representative be knowledgeable about the general education curriculum. This will allow the LEA representative to help the general and special education teachers on the IEP team to consider how a student can work within the general curriculum.

Ideally the LEA representative will be a good listener, who after hearing the thoughts and concerns of all IEP team members, will make sure that the IEP itself is carried out. The LEA representative may also be responsible for seeing that a number of legal requirements regarding the IEP team are followed.

The LEA representative brings to the IEP team meeting:

- ▸ Knowledge of the whole general education curriculum and sequence of courses.
- ▸ Knowledge about how the general education curriculum relates to special education and related services.
- ▸ Experience in collaboration.
- ▸ Knowledge of general issues such as staff teaching strengths, class sizes, and outside issues that impact the teaching and learning process.
- ▸ Knowledge of resources that are available.
- ▸ Knowledge of the student in different contexts, for example, at lunch, at dances, and during sports. Who does the student sit with at lunch? How does the student act when everyone is asked to line up? Who are this student's friends? Who plays with the student on the playground?

In order to participate in the IEP process, the LEA representative needs to learn how to

- ▸ Frame the discussion in terms of each student's unique educational needs.
- ▸ Negotiate effectively with all parties.
- ▸ Make sure that no team member is harassed or treated unfairly.
- ▸ Promote a productive collaborative effort among team members to carry out the IEP.

The Parents

The view of parents and their vision for their child's future is crucial to the development of a meaningful IEP that will help students move beyond the school environment. Although there has always been a role for parents in the IEP process, Congress was concerned that parents have not been adequately supported and encouraged to express their needs and hopes for their children. A central question, then, is "How can schools support parents to be more active partners?"

IDEA '97 strengthened parental involvement in the following ways:

▸ Parents must be given the opportunity to participate in any meetings about the identification, evaluation, and educational placement of their son or daughter. In this regard, "meetings" mean prearranged events, not unscheduled or informal conversations among school staff.

▸ Parents must be invited to team meetings to determine what additional information is needed for a student's evaluation, to determine a student's eligibility for special education, or to consider the educational placement of a student.

▸ The parents' concerns, as well as the information they provide about students, must be considered when developing and reviewing the IEP.

▸ Parents must give their permission for both student evaluations and re-evaluations. The requirement regarding reevaluations is new. Parental permission must be obtained unless the school can demonstrate that it took reasonable steps to obtain the consent, but the parent did not respond.

▸ Parents must be informed, on a report card or its equivalent, about their child's progress toward meeting annual IEP goals. The schools must report this information to the parents at least as often as it sends out report cards to the parents of students without disabilities.

IDEA '97 requires that one or both parents of a student with a disability are present at each IEP meeting or, at the least, are given the chance to participate. The school or district must

▸ Notify parents of an IEP meeting "early enough to ensure that they will have an opportunity to attend." This notice must include the purpose, time, and location of the meeting, as well as a list of people who will be there.

Schedule the meeting at a mutually agreed upon time and place.

▸ Find other ways for parents to participate if they cannot attend, such as individual or conference telephone calls.

▸ Do whatever is necessary to make sure that parents understand what's going on at the meeting, including arranging for an interpreter.

▸ Keep records of attempts to contact the parents if the parents declined to attend the IEP team meeting, but the meeting was held anyway.

IDEA has other requirements regarding parents as well, and also spells out procedures for parents to follow when they disagree with IEP team or school decisions. Check out your own state and district requirements if you have any questions about the roles and rights of parents.

As a teacher and IEP team member, you can help parents to become more active and skilled in contributing to their child's IEP. Emphasize the fact that fresh, up-to-date parental observations about the student's progress, struggles, and accomplishments will help the team to design an effective educational program. Draw on your own expertise, or on the skills of other team members, to teach parents how to observe their children objectively and to record their observations. Consult the information later in this chapter regarding Guidelines for Behavioral Observation. *Negotiating The Special Education Maze: A Guide for Parents and Teachers* (Anderson et al., 1997) describes how parents can observe their children, and provides sample forms that parents can use to record and organize their observations.

A final exercise for parents is to identify their own short- and long-term goals for the child. What would make life easier at home in the short run? What do they see as legitimate goals for the student's educational program? What do they expect from the student?

The Student

Central to the IEP team meeting is the presence of the student. It is important for students to know that this is their team, their meeting, and that the team is gathered to discuss their present and future. Students need to be helped to express as much self-determination as possible and to share their vision for the future. By law, the student is included as part of the IEP team "if appropriate." When the purpose of the IEP meeting is to consider needed transition services, the student must be invited (see Chapter 12).

Levels and kinds of student participation in the IEP meeting will differ by age and disposition. For example, a high school student might work closely with the IEP team to plan for post-high school education or employment. On the other hand, a restless 7-year-old may only stay for 5 minutes. But there are reasons why even young children might attend, even if they don't stay the whole time. They are the focus of the discussions, and they should have an opportunity to comment. By attending at least part of the meeting, the student will become acquainted with the circle of adults who form that student's support system. They will learn who is "on their team," who understands their strengths and needs, and who they can approach for help.

If the student will be attending the IEP meeting, someone should talk with the student beforehand about who will be there, what will be discussed, questions she might be asked, and what information that she can offer. Student thoughts and preferences can be conveyed to the group in a variety of ways, for example, in writing, through portfolios, or though pictures. Rehearse with the student and show her where she will sign the document.

Or, the student can convey her preferences and interests to a selected participant and that person can share the information with the group. Give the student a choice, but encourage active participation, since this can be part of a move toward independent living. Even young students can provide useful information to the IEP team. For example, if the team is designing positive strategies to deal with disruptive behavior, a student may offer reasons why she acts in one way or another, and this can be helpful to the group.

There are important reasons for students to get more involved with their IEPs. At different locations around the country, we have heard stories about students leading their own IEP meetings and writing portions of their IEPs themselves. This is a way for students to gain confidence, to learn to speak up for themselves, to understand their own strengths and their needs, and to explain those strengths and needs to others. Educators report that parents are more likely to attend student-led IEP team meetings, and that the meetings themselves tend to be more positive and student centered.

Leaders in the field believe that the student-led IEP is an excellent way for students to acquire "self-determination skills," or the ability to set and achieve goals based on self-knowledge. Current research indicates that people who are "self-determined" are more likely to be employed and to earn higher wages than those who lack this quality. To locate more information about self-determination skills, see Appendix II.

One point to remember: If the student is at the meeting, team members need to remember to talk to the student (and not just to each other about the student as if the student weren't there). The participants also need to use words and terms that the student understands. In preparing for an IEP team meeting, you may want to think about how the student can communicate (for example, verbally, in written form, through a survey or interview, or with pictures):

- ▸ What the student likes to do and can do.
- ▸ What the student prefers not doing.
- ▸ What the student would like to learn.
- ▸ Whether the student wishes to bring friend(s) to discuss what the student can or cannot do.
- ▸ What the student needs for future goals.
- ▸ Where the student would like to go to school, work, or live.
- ▸ In what leisure and recreation activities would the student like to participate.

Guidelines for Behavioral Observation

Behavioral observation of students should

1. Be systematic and take place in a variety of settings.

2. Be done by different IEP team members.

3. Provide a clear picture of the behavior using one or more of the following procedures:

- ▶ Narrative recording that describes specific skills the student demonstrates, the types of directions the student responds to best, social interactions, and personal appearance.

- ▶ Time sampling or interval recording that examines whether or not a specific behavior is occurring at predetermined intervals (for example, every 2 minutes). A disadvantage of time sampling is that it does not reflect the frequency of behaviors on an ongoing basis.

- ▶ Event sampling that waits for a specific behavior to occur and then records the frequency and duration of the behavior. A disadvantage may be that the student fails to exhibit the targeted behavior, such as social interaction.

- ▶ Rating scales that provide a more structured technique to observe and record behaviors.

Assess for Success: Handbook on Transition Assessment provides more detailed information on these and other techniques for observing student behavior. See Appendix II for more information about this publication (Sitlington, Neubert, Begun, Lombard, & Leconte, 1996).

Other Members of the IEP Team

Three additional categories of people who need to represented at the IEP team meeting:

1. *Someone who is qualified to discuss the "instructional implications of evaluation results."* Someone on the IEP team needs to know which evaluations of the student have been conducted, the results, and the consequences for instructional purposes. This person is not necessarily a diagnostician, or the person who conducted the tests, but may be another knowledgeable member of the team.

It's important to know not only evaluation results and test data, but also descriptions of the student's behavior during testing, any expressed feelings of confidence or frustration, tolerance handling a new situation, interaction with the evaluator (authority figure), and the student's strengths and needs.

The evaluation person needs to be able to:

▸ Explain why an evaluation was done and which areas (such as study skills or reading level) were evaluated.
▸ Explain the evaluation results clearly so that all participants can understand.
▸ Specify which test results indicate a need for intervention or monitoring of student progress.
▸ Explain which test results point to a need for special education services or accommodations in the general education classroom.
▸ Indicate what kind of instruction, instructional strategies, materials, and environments might help meet the student's needs.

2. *Agency representatives to assist with transition planning.* If a purpose of the meeting is to plan for a student's transition out of high school, then the school will invite a representative of any agency that is likely to provide or pay for transition services. The team needs to consider: Who can help with transition planning? Help provide access to the community? Conduct vocational evaluations? What agencies can or will be providing services to the student after high school? Keep in mind that important transition services commence years before high school graduation.

If an agency or organization declines the invitation to attend an IEP meeting, then other steps must be taken to obtain the participation of the agency in the planning of any transition services. More information about transition planning is found in Chapter 12 of this book.

3. *Other people who are invited by the school or the parents to join the IEP team.* Either the school or a parent may invite additional people to join the IEP team. For example, the school may invite an additional teacher, a school psychologist, or a specialist whose expertise is needed. If the LEA representative on the IEP team does not feel fully knowledgeable about the general education curriculum, he or she might want to bring someone else. If the school does invite extra people, it must let the parents know about this in advance.

Be sure that the parents know that they, too, may bring anyone of their choosing to the IEP team meeting. This could be someone to help the parents listen, understand, ask questions, explain special issues, or take notes. For example, the parents could invite a friend or mentor, a counselor, a member of the clergy, a legal advisor, a professional advocate, or a nurse. You can ask the parents to notify the school, as a courtesy, if they are bringing their own guests to the IEP meeting.

Chapter 4
The IEP Team as a Team

The process for developing IEPs is unique in some ways. But it has also has aspects that are probably familiar to you. You may find it helpful to "survive" the ups and downs of the process if you've spent a little time thinking about what makes the IEP team both like and different from other kinds of teams that you have been part of.

How is the IEP team different from some other teams?

- There is a legal framework of required relationships among the partners. Federal, state, and local laws and policies spell out in some detail who must participate and what they must do. This is especially true for the school district, which has many legal responsibilities regarding the education of students with disabilities.
- The team members share both responsibility and accountability for the success of the student in meeting his goals.
- The process is "results oriented," meaning that what matters is not how happy everyone is with the process, but the success of the student's educational program.

The team must reach consensus or go to mediation or due process procedures. The objective is to develop an educational program for the student. But in any case, the team must find a way to come to closure, even if all parties "agree to disagree." Chapter 13 describes what happens when the IEP team members cannot agree.

- The team has the challenge of meeting its responsibilities to the student while conducting meetings that are of a reasonable length, given people's other responsibilities at the job and at home. The team can't meet forever with no resolution.
- The team must maintain a balance between the "head" (what law requires them to do) and the "heart" (the welfare and success of the student), although these factors should support each other.
- The IEP team process must somehow integrate the diverse perspectives of teachers, parents, students, school officials, and others into a singular focus on and agreement about the unique needs of each student.
- The IEP creates unique solutions based on the particular needs of each individual student with disabilities. This is not a "cookie cutter" process in any respect.

▶   The IEP process is built on a vision of schooling as an individualized process that aims not just for high school graduation, but for the student's ability to be an independent, responsible, constructive member of society and to live a satisfying life.

The IEP process starts by considering and emphasizing the student's strengths and builds onward from there.

▶   The team is involved in more than a one-time event. Rather, it is part of an ongoing process and relationship among the different parties who are involved in it.

The quality of IEP team members' relationship is a crucial factor in its success. This requires trust and respect. Assume that everyone at the table has a different vision and perspective, and that there are many important perspectives. Each must be carefully considered.

The IEP meeting is a time to share observations and perspectives and to listen carefully to one another, especially to the student, the parents, and the teachers. At an initial IEP meeting, in particular, it is important to listen carefully to the people that the student knows. Combining perspectives, the group attains a combined picture of all points of view. In the end, the team's task is to integrate the diverse perspectives of its members as part of an ongoing process and relationship.

Centering the meeting around discussions of the student's strengths and needs will create a positive atmosphere that can strengthen the student's self-respect. No one wants to attend a meeting in which other people center their comments on what one *can't* do. Creating an atmosphere where students are encouraged to speak out for themselves builds confidence.

The team is responsible for designing services and solutions that are *appropriate* for the student. Appropriate solutions do not necessarily require the most expensive or intensive technology or services that the team can dream up, particularly when the student must be pulled out of the general education classroom to use them. Appropriate solutions support the student's struggle for independent functioning and his ability to be, to the maximum extent possible, part of the mainstream education experience. There will always be a tension between wanting to meet all of the student's needs, on one hand, and challenging the student to meet his goals of becoming independent. Sometimes this means providing *fewer* services rather than more. But the team must carefully weigh these issues, in order to make sure that any essential services are provided to the student.

The challenge is to keep pulling back to the student's needs: "What goals do we have for this student and how best can he get there?" There aren't always easy answers to this question. Often the team must make an educated "best guess" and try something new. The new strategy may fail, but then the team learns from its mistake and tries again. An important point is for all team members, including the special and general educators and parents, to reach consensus about where to go.

It might help you to reflect upon the other kinds of teams that you are a part of (Friend & Cook, 1996). For example, three important kinds of teams in day-to-day life are found in families, among friends, and at work. People divide up into different kinds of teams in schools. In general, teams are formed to pool resources, divide up work, and to safeguard against individual errors in judgment. Most teams can have the following kinds of characteristics:

▸ A perception shared among team members and recognized by outsiders that "this is a functioning team."
▸ Spoken or unspoken expectations of one another; for example, being on time or using "lay" language when parents are present.
▸ More or less interdependence. If one person is missing, can the group still function?

Effective teams are characterized by:

▸ Clear goals and processes that everyone understands.
▸ Individual feelings of being included, respected, and valued, as well as a sense that the team process is more satisfying than frustrating.
▸ Responsibilities and accountability for what each team member is expected to contribute.
▸ Shared responsibility for conducting the various parts of the meeting, for example, initiating discussion, encouraging, summarizing, and gaining consensus.

Effective teams are often described as "collaborative." A team may or may not act collaboratively, depending on the personal relationships among the team members. In order for collaboration to work, the following kinds of characteristics are important:

▸ Participation is voluntary. The fact that IEP teams are mandatory and their membership is spelled out by law can work against a collaborative spirit.
▸ Parity among participants. The IEP process unites the family, school, and community as partners. Every team member is important and has something important to contribute.
▸ Mutual goals. All team member's goals may not be the same, but they need to share some goals. In the case of the IEP, the goal is an appropriate program for the student.
▸ Shared responsibility for making decisions.
▸ The sharing of resources such as time, information, and special skills.
▸ Shared accountability for the outcomes of the team's efforts, whether those results are positive or negative.

Some aspects of an IEP team's negotiations may work against collaboration. For example, an LEA representative may feel pressured because of budget constraints to resist providing some expensive services. A teacher might feel pressured to provide services that he or she feels are unreasonable, causing him or her to resist cooperating with other team members.

Parents may feel pressured to approve a decision that they do not believe to be in the best interest of their child.

A skilled chairperson for the IEP team can make the process much easier. The chairperson is not specified by IDEA and thus may be any member of the IEP team. The chairperson should be someone who can facilitate, mediate, and encourage the participation of all IEP team members. The chairperson sets the tone of the meeting and helps the team stay positive, considerate, and focused on the task at hand.

Chapter 5
Preparing for an IEP Team Meeting

The IEP team meeting is more likely to run smoothly if all team members are adequately prepared to participate. First of all, every team member should know the following definitions contained within IDEA; this is the framework for their work:

- *The general curriculum* — the curriculum that applies to *all* students within the school district or school, whether they have disabilities or not. This term relates to what students learn and *not* to the setting in which they learn it. The general curriculum can be used in any educational setting.
- *Specially designed instruction* — an adaptation of content, methodology, or delivery of instruction to address the unique needs resulting from a student's disability and to ensure access of the student to the general curriculum, so that she can meet the educational standards that apply to all students.

Participants should also know what must be included in the IEP, which is listed at the end of Chapter 2.

To prepare for the IEP meeting, team members need to be ready to discuss the student's "present level of performance." *All* participants must be prepared to describe from their perspective the student's present level of functioning using means such as

- Portfolios of work.
- Lists of strengths and accomplishments, academic and nonacademic.
- Observations of behavior, social interactions, and developmental achievements.
- Observations of instructional strategies and learning environments (such as a quiet room or preferred seating arrangement) that work well.
- Test results, including performance assessments and authentic assessments.
- A description of areas of need and the effect of the disability on academic and nonacademic achievements.

Participants should use descriptive statements that are

- Specific. "Jay multiplies two digit numbers correctly 90% of the time using a calculator."
- Positive. "Judy can independently follow two-step verbal directions."

- ► Complete. "Elizabeth copies simple shapes (circles, squares, and triangles) with a crayon on butcher block paper."
- ► Accurate. "When given the utensils, Darren can set up to four place settings at a table with minimal verbal prompting."

Team participants will need to use this information to help them to figure out if the student's disability affects her involvement and progress in the general education curriculum.

Preparing Positive Descriptions of Student Behavior

Here is a list of verbs and phrases that may help you to prepare positive descriptive statements:

attentive	cooperative	follows multi-step directions
alert	well-mannered	
calm	helpful	requires repetition of directions
cheerful	thinks before acting	
well-groomed	uses trial and error approach	ignores distractions
coordinated	orderly	needs time to transition
makes appropriate eye contact	deliberate	asks for help
understandable speech	persistent	recognizes errors
animated	inquisitive	able to spell
spontaneous	variable motivation level	creatively spells
fluent	accepts mistakes	memorizes words
engaging	adaptable	passive learner
articulate	transitions well	actively involved in learning
thoughtful	learns from doing	requires information in a variety of modes
open	notes detail	needs visual cues
stays on task	willing to try again	requires auditory cues
consistent	applies him- or herself	requires preparation for transition
goal-directed	shows effort	
takes initiative	follows one-step directions	
	follows two-step directions	

It's an old story, but one worth repeating: The work that goes on in advance of a meeting greatly influences the quality of the meeting. IDEA requires that the parents be informed of the purpose, time, and location of the meeting, as well as a list of people who will be there. In addition, we suggest that the invitation list the goals of the meeting and decisions that need to be made, including specific topics to be discussed. You may even want to create a draft agenda, along with questions to consider in advance. Be sure to include any written material that the meeting participants need to discuss.

These are the kinds of things you'll want to think about before an IEP meeting:

- Have the participants been provided with information or training about the IEP process?
- Have the participants been identified and invited and their roles and duties defined?
- Has a chairperson been appointed?
- If appropriate, has the student been invited to attend?
- If it is suspected that extensive services are needed by the student, is the LEA or agency representative knowledgeable about and in a position to authorize these services?
- Has there been prior communication with everyone involved in the student's educational program? Does this include electives? Sometimes teachers of elective subjects are not contacted, but a student strength could be found in music, art, computers, or physical education. You might find it valuable to send out forms to every teacher that a student has.
- Is classroom coverage provided for teachers who will attend?
- Are all necessary forms and supplies available?
- Will the meeting place accommodate all participants and be a comfortable and quiet place to work?

This checklist will help you to evaluate whether you have met your legal obligations regarding parents:

- Have we notified the parents of an IEP meeting early enough to ensure that they will have an opportunity to attend?
- Have we informed the parents of the purpose, time, and location of the meeting, as well as a list of people who will be there?
- Have we scheduled the meeting at a mutually agreed upon time and place?
- If the parents couldn't participate in the meeting, did we try to find other ways for them to participate, such as individual or conference telephone calls?
- Have we done whatever was necessary to make sure that parents will understand what is going on at the meeting, including arranging for an interpreter?
- Have we kept records of attempts to contact the parents if the parents declined to attend the IEP team meeting, but the meeting was held anyway?

These are additional factors to consider about parent involvement:

- If a letter was sent, did it include the purpose of the meeting in language understandable to the parents?
- Have we addressed the best ways to contact and encourage the participation of parents from typically underrepresented groups (i.e., ethnically, culturally, and linguistically diverse groups)?
- When choosing a meeting place, did we consider its convenience, accessibility, and alternative locations to increase the likelihood of parent participation?

▸ How did we prepare the parents for the IEP meeting? Has the parent received information related to the IEP process?

How can we help the parents to:

▸ Bring information that will add to an understanding of their child (e.g., medical reports, educational reports, letters from family, friends, and community members)?
▸ Provide a history of their child's physical, educational, and social development?
▸ Provide information about their child and be prepared to share their vision and goals?
▸ Explain perceived problems and behaviors at home, and describe interventions that work?
▸ List or talk about their child's strengths and interests and describe the environments where these strengths are exhibited?
▸ Provide information about their child's needs and identify what services they believe are needed to maximize abilities?
▸ Identify people to come with them to the meeting (such as a parent mentor or friend)?
▸ Have we been flexible in scheduling the time for the meeting for parents who work or have other commitments (e.g., have we offered early morning, lunchtime, or evening meetings)?

It helps if each team member has questions to think about in advance, to focus their thoughts. We intend to assist you in the sections that follow by listing the kinds of questions that different IEP team members might need to think about before attending a meeting. Questions such as these could be typed out and distributed to team members several weeks before the meeting, so that everyone has time to prepare for a discussion.

General Education Teacher:

▸ What are the student's strengths?
▸ What is the general education curriculum? What are the state and local educational standards? Where is the student functioning within these?
▸ Is the student participating in state and local assessments? If yes, how is she faring?
▸ What kind of goals and benchmarks might be important for this student?
▸ What learning and instructional strategies and environments work best for this student?
▸ What kind of support or help might be important for the student?
▸ What kind of support would help *me* to assist this student?
▸ What kind of assistance or information could the family and student provide?
▸ Does the student have any behavior issues we should be addressing?

Special Educators and Related Services Providers:

- What are the student's strengths?
- Where is the student functioning within the context of the general education curriculum?
- How is the student faring with the general education state and/or local assessments?
- What kind of goals and benchmarks do I have for this student?
- What progress has this student made?
- What can I do to help this student's performance to improve?
- Is the student receiving the appropriate and necessary accommodations and modifications?
- How can the family reinforce what this student is learning at school?
- Do we need assistance from other persons or agencies?
- How can we address any behavior issues the student may have?

LEA Representative:

- Have I reviewed this student's file?
- What is the general education curriculum, and what are the district standards and assessments that apply to this student?
- What options and resources can the district offer in support of this student?
- Am I authorized to commit these resources?
- Are the supports in place that will allow this student's teachers to attend the IEP team meeting?
- What kind of help could the rest of the building staff offer to this student and family?

Family:

- What does my child do well?
- What does my child struggle with?
- What are my long-range goals for my son or daughter?
- What skills would increase the independence of my son or daughter?
- What goals would strengthen us as a family?
- Are there transportation or mobility issues?
- What do I want the school to do for my child?
- What particular things do I want the school to report to me about?
- What should I know to be able to support my child's progress at school and in the home?
- How and when are good times for the school to contact me when this is necessary? What if there is an emergency or crisis?
- How can I communicate with the school? Should I send notes? Who and when should I call?
- What information should I give to the school on an ongoing basis?

Student:

- What am I good at doing?
- What is hard for me to do?
- What do I like to do?
- What do I want to accomplish right now? What skills will I need? How might I get them? What help will I need?
- What works well for me in the general education class? Am I experiencing any problems?
- What do I want to be when I grow up?

Evaluation Person:

- What are the student's strengths?
- What are the implications of the evaluation results for the student's educational program?
- Has the parent been given copies of all evaluations prior to the meeting?
- Has the parent had a chance to discuss these evaluations with relevant personnel?

Agency Representatives Involved in Transition Planning:

- What do I know about the strengths and goals of this student?
- Starting at age 14 (or earlier), what course of study will help the student reach her long-term goals?
- What services can my agency offer?
- What am I authorized to offer and what kinds of commitments am I authorized to make on behalf of my agency?
- How might my agency cooperate or link with other agencies to provide support?

Other People Invited by the Parents or the School:

- What are the student's strengths?
- What are the student's interests?
- How do I think that this student learns best?
- Under what circumstances have I observed this student being successful?
- What kinds of support would help this student be successful in the future?
- How can I help?

A final consideration when preparing for the meeting: When it is time to reevaluate a student, the IEP team now may decide if it needs additional information about the student. In other words, the team is no longer required to complete a "full and comprehensive" evaluation of student factors that had been assessed before. If the team decides that no new information is needed, then it must notify the parents and tell them that they have the right to a full and comprehensive evaluation if they want one.

Chapter 6
Assessing the Present Level of Educational Performance and Developing Measurable Goals, Short-Term Objectives, and Benchmarks

Up to this point, we have discussed the IEP and IEP team in general terms, as well as how to prepare for an IEP team meeting. Now, we will begin to review what needs to be accomplished at the meeting itself.

Although the IEP meeting typically starts with establishing a student's level of educational performance and progress within the general education curriculum, it is essential to spend some time creating a vision for the student's future, one that the student and her family see as important. It is helpful to write down some broad "life goals" to keep before the team enabling them to determine whether the specified IEP goals and objectives will help the student reach her desired destination. Full consideration of the student's strengths and needs, as well as the parents' concerns and goals, should drive this process. All of the information that was gathered before the meeting, including any evaluation data, is used to understand the student's level of performance.

You will also want to consider how the student is progressing in meeting any state or local standards for education. These standards usually are, broadly speaking, either "content standards" (describing what a student should know) or "performance standards" (describing what a student should know how to do to meet the standards). Education standards vary quite a bit from location to location, but the general education teacher and curriculum specialists will know what kind of standards exist in your school district.

The statement of present levels of achievement should accurately describe the effect of the student's disability on her performance in any area of education that is affected, including (1) academic areas, (2) nonacademic areas such as daily life activities or mobility, (3) physical education, and if applicable, (4) transition. The statement should be written in objective measurable terms, to the extent possible.

There should be a direct relationship between the present levels of educational performance and the other components of the IEP. Thus, if the IEP describes a problem with the student's reading level and points to a deficiency in a specific reading skill, this problem should be addressed under goals, short-term objectives or benchmarks, and specific education and related services to be provided to the student.

You may wish to consider questions such as these when developing a student's present level of performance:

- Do the "present levels of performance" clearly provide a "snapshot"of the student? Would anyone be able to begin instruction or intervention?
- Are the present levels understandable so that goals may easily be developed?
- Are all appropriate areas addressed (such as language, motor development, and behavior)?
- What skills has the student acquired? What needs to be acquired?
- Has the IEP team addressed the student's strengths, needs, and experiences, when appropriate, especially for transition?
- Have long-range plans for the student been discussed or reviewed?

Once the present level of achievement has been established, the group will move on to setting goals, benchmarks, and short-term objectives for the student. The goals

- Are annual goals that describe what a student can reasonably be expected to accomplish within a 12-month period.
- Should be developed for each critical area of need identified in the "present levels of educational performance."
- Must be measurable. The word "measurable" was added in IDEA '97. Measurable goals are easier to assess. This change was intended to make the goals clearer for teachers, parents, and the student.
- Must meet the student's needs that result from her disability and *enable him or her to be involved in and progress in the general curriculum.*
- Meet each of the student's other educational needs that result from her disability.

In setting goals, one considers:

- *Who* will achieve?
- *What* measurable, observable skill or behavior?
- *When*? By what time or on what date?

Each goal should be a specific, positive statement. For example, these would not be good goals, because they are not really measurable:

- John will strengthen his writing skills this year.
- Sengeeta will learn to work more independently.
- Garrett will learn to count.

Notice that these goals are more specific:

- By June 1, John will plan, draft, revise, proofread, and edit a two-page book report.
- By June 1, Sengeeta will work on her homework for half an hour each afternoon without prompting.

▸   By June 1, Garrett will count by ones to 20.

The student's goals should be tied to the state or district's educational standards for all students, as much as is appropriate. (McIntire, 1997b). But it is not possible (nor should IEP teams feel compelled to) address in any given year every content or performance standard that a district has. Rather, the IEP team needs to

▸   Identify and prioritize the standards that will address the individual learning needs of a particular student.
▸   Discuss the general education teacher's priorities in terms of the knowledge and skills that students without disabilities should acquire in a particular year.
▸   Discuss what knowledge and skills the student with disabilities should be able to acquire, and needs to acquire, with special education support.
▸   Use this information to develop goals, benchmarks, and objectives that will be used to show the student's progress in achieving his goals.

The Congress had this to say (*Senate Report*, IDEA '97):

> "The new emphasis on participation in the general education curriculum is not intended by the committee to result in major expansions in the size of the IEP of dozens of pages of detailed goals and benchmarks or objectives in every curricular content standard or skill. The new focus is intended to produce attention to the general education curriculum."

Once you have written goals for the student, then you will move on to consider benchmarks or short-term objectives. Short-term objectives or benchmarks

▸   Are the intermediate steps necessary to reach the long-range goals. They are the steps or milestones between the "present level of performance" and the "annual goal."
▸   Contain the same basic parts as annual goals — the "who," "what," and "when."
▸   Provide a way for teachers, parents, and students to understand whether the student is making progress.

You may write either benchmarks or short-term objectives. But what is the difference between them? "Benchmark" was a new term introduced within IDEA '97; before that time, IEP teams were required to write "short-term objectives." This has been a bit confusing, especially since the term "benchmarks" means different things to different people. In IDEA '97, benchmarks and short-term objectives serve the same purpose, but benchmarks are broader statements.

Short-term objectives tend to center on very specific skills. For example:

▸   A benchmark: "By January, Marcus will multiply three-place decimals."

▸   A short-term objective: "By January, Marcus will be able to multiply up to three-place decimals with 80% accuracy as demonstrated by solving 10 teacher-generated problems on three separate occasions."

Here is an example of an annual goal and benchmarks:

Annual Goal (in the area of 10th grade mathematics)
    Marcus will divide three-place decimals by June 1.

Present Level of Performance:
    Marcus can multiply one-place decimals.

Benchmark:
    By November, Marcus will multiply two-place decimals.

Benchmark:
    By January, Marcus will multiply three-place decimals.

Benchmark:
    By March, Marcus will divide two-place decimals.

These goals and benchmarks are specific, measurable, and concrete. They describe the year's goal and the steps for Marcus to get there. Teachers, the student, and the parents will be able to tell, by particular dates, whether Marcus is making good progress toward meeting his yearly goal.

Your team can choose to use either short-term objectives or benchmarks. Benchmarks are broader and can be easier to write. Using benchmarks can simplify the IEP process and yet allow teachers and parents to assess the progress of a student in attaining goals. But the benchmarks should not be too broad, as they provide a basis for tracking progress and assuring accountability.

Some people may decide to continue using short-term objectives, since they provide more detail for teachers and parents who prefer this. The disadvantage arises when there are too many very specific objectives, which can be confusing and difficult to manage. And for some IEP teams, the question may not be whether or not to have short-term objectives, it may be whether or not to put them into the IEP.

Benchmarks and objectives can be understood as a kind of ladder, in which the student advances rung by rung to more advanced skills and concepts. But there's a problem with this view. Some students may stay at lower benchmarks because they can't master them — and as a result, never get exposed to higher level skills and information. There is an old story to illustrate this problem, in which a student never learns about the existence of World War I because he didn't master the Civil War. He didn't have the skills to finish the reading.

In creating goals, benchmarks, and objectives — and at other points in the IEP process — you will need to think about accommodations and modifications.

- *Accommodations* are supports or services provided to help students progress in the general education curriculum and demonstrate their learning. These do not mean big changes in the instructional level, content, or standards. Rather, support is provided so that students have an equal opportunity to learn and to demonstrate what they have learned.

- *Modifications* change the content and performance expectations for what a student should learn. For example, a student may work at a different level (for example, at a 4th grade level instead of a 6th grade level in reading) or study fewer concepts or skills.

How might you use accommodations and modifications when setting goals and benchmarks? The following example will illustrate this and, at the same time, explain how you can set goals that are tied to general education standards.

Peter is a fourth grader who has a learning disability in the area of reading. One standard for Grades 3 through 5 in his district is that students should be able to "Read to organize and integrate information for a purpose." For example, students of that age are expected to know how to paraphrase, organize information for reports, and make comparisons.

Peter's IEP team has adopted the standard mentioned as one annual goal, and they have written "benchmarks" to track his progress. These benchmarks are:

- Peter will read and take notes on an article at an upper elementary level using an outline by November.
- Peter will complete a three-paragraph research paper on a given topic by January.
- Peter will compare and contrast two authors and state an opinion about each by March.

Achievement of these benchmarks will help Peter to meet the general education standard. The content of the reading curriculum may have to be *modified* to support his progress. In other subjects, he may need *accommodations* (such as a change in the delivery of instruction, given his reading disability) in order to progress.

The IEP team needs to examine the standards and content areas in the general education curriculum and ask which the student can achieve:

- Without accommodations? For example, Peter requires no accommodations for instructional activities that don't involve reading.
- With accommodations? When classroom activities require reading, Peter will need highlighted copies of books and study materials.

- ▸ Will need to be modified or addressed individually on the IEP? Peter's reading program needs to be modified and should be limited to concentration on the *big ideas* central to each lesson.
- ▸ Will need to be modified but does not need to be addressed individually on the IEP? Peter will use books and other resources from the library as part of his general education experience.
- ▸ Will need to be expanded or individualized? Peter will keep a portfolio that shows his understanding of the *big ideas* in each book he reads.

The last question above, regarding "expanded or individualized" standards or content areas, would most often apply to students with more severe disabilities. In these cases, students would work toward the general education standards, but the meaning of the standard might be expanded to include more basic and functional skills. These are students for whom the general education curriculum, even when modified in level or content, will not meet their needs. For example, one district modified a geography standard to mean achievement of physical mobility for a student with severe disabilities. This kind of alteration would be needed for only a small percentage of students with disabilities.

Yet another consideration when adapting general education standards has to do with their nature and specificity. When standards are very challenging, specific, and academic, only the highest-achieving students may fully meet them. On the other hand, broader standards may allow flexibility for different students to demonstrate mastery. For example, a student with mild mental retardation may demonstrate his ability to use numbers in a way that meets the state standard — a standard that challenges this particular student to achieve at his highest level. Also, standards may or may not address life and career skills that are applicable to all students. You will need to examine the nature of your own state and district standards to understand how well they will fit the needs of individual students with disabilities.

We have been discussing accommodations and modifications in regard to goals, benchmarks, and objectives, but they may be reflected in other parts of the IEP. The team needs to address accommodations needed in each class or extracurricular activity. It should think about whether a student needs accommodations in instruction, assessment, classroom organization and management, access to technology, homework, study-work aids, and assistive technology.

The chart on page 47 is intended to help you to visualize how you can use general education standards as annual goals when you are developing the IEP. You would begin this process, as always, by establishing the student's present level of performance to understand the student's strengths and the areas where he is struggling and needs assistance.

Next, the team would consider which general education standards to include as annual goals for the student on the IEP. In most cases, states and districts have many standards in many subject areas. Therefore, we are assuming that it is not possible, practical, or even necessary to include every general education standard as an annual goal for the student. Rather, the IEP team would identify *which* general education standards the student is having trouble mastering and adopt those as goals. If the student is struggling to master many general education standards, the IEP team would decide which standards would be a *priority* for the student to work toward in a given year.

After the team has decided which general education standards should serve as annual goals for the student, it must determine whether the student can work toward the standards as written or if the standard will need to be modified. In many cases, the students can work toward the same educational standards as students without disabilities. In other instances, the team will need to modify the standard so that it is an appropriate goal for an individual student.

If the team decides that a student can work toward a general education standard without any change or modification, then it writes benchmarks or short-term objectives that spell out the steps toward meeting that goal. That is, the team describes what intermediate levels of progress toward meeting the goal that the student should achieve by what dates. The team also must figure out what accommodations, special instruction, and services the school will provide to help the student reach his goals and benchmarks.

On the other hand, the team may decide that it needs to change or modify a general education standard. For example, a student may need to work toward standards that apply for a different grade level — fourth grade reading standards instead of eighth grade reading standards, for example. A smaller number of students have disabilities that significantly interfere with their ability to meet general education standards. Their IEPs may focus on other priorities, such as long-term independence skills. For these students, the general education standards may have to be significantly altered. When the general education standards have been modified as necessary, then the team would write benchmarks or short-term objectives and determine the accommodations, special instruction, and services that the student would receive.

Accommodations

This is a list of accommodations developed by the Aurora, Colorado, Public Schools (Poulson & Fognani-Smaus). Many other accommodations are effective, as well. Contact The Council for Exceptional Children to obtain more information about effective accommodations for particular disabilities.

Assessment

Read assessment orally to student
Adapt format of assessments
Open book assessments
Oral or taped responses
Reduce reading level on assessments
Reduce number of items

Instructional Strategies

Multisensory approaches
Whole word approach to teaching reading
Linguistic approach to teaching reading
Rebus instructions and/or reading
Language experience approach
Concrete materials and manipulatives
Hands-on experiences
Repeat/rephrase directions
Braille
Recorded books
Self-checking materials
Programmed materials
High interest/low vocabulary reading

Study/Work Aids

Student to tape lecture
Student to type assignments
Access to taped library books and novels
Highlighted copies of study guides
Highlighted copies of textbooks
Vocabulary files for courses
Visual cues in textbooks/worksheets
Visual cues with lecture
Adjust length of assignments

Additional time for assignments
Adapted worksheets
Study guides
Progress charts
Colored acetate for contrast
Abacus
Slant board

Classroom Organization and Management

Predictable structure and routine
Preferential seating
Contingency/behavior contract
Level system
Time-out space or room
Prepare for transitions
Positive reinforcement
Frequent feedback
Consistent expectations and consequences
Immediate feedback

Access to Technology

Large print display
Calculator
Typewriter
Tape recorder
Brailler
Scanner or reader
Computer with word processor
CCTV
Communication device
Word prediction software
Auditory trainer
Overhead projector

The Decision-Making Process: How Do I Use General Education Standards to Develop the IEP?

Begin by establishing the student's present level of performance.

▼

Then look at your district's education standards and decide which standards the student will have difficulty mastering because of his disability and are most important for the student to master. This will help you to decide which standards need to be addressed in the student's IEP.

▼

The IEP standards that will be addressed can be used as annual goals for the student. But first, you must decide if the student can work toward a particular standard as written or if the standard will need to be modified.

▼ ▼

Yes, the student can work toward the standard as written.

No, the student cannot work toward the standard as written.

▼ ▼

Use the standard as an annual goal on the IEP and develop benchmarks.

Modify the standard in content or level, as appropriate. (For a few students with more severe disabilities, you may need to substantially alter or individualize the standard.)

▼ ▼

Describe any accommodations, special instruction, and services that the student will need to meet the standard and benchmarks.

Use the modified standard as an annual goal on the IEP and develop benchmarks.

▼

Describe any accommodations, special instruction, and services that the student will need to meet the standard and benchmarks.

Chapter 7
Providing Access to the General Education Curriculum:
Special Education, Related Services, and Supplementary Aids and Services

The next section that needs to be included in the IEP describes what support and services the school will provide so that a student with disabilities can work within the general education curriculum. These are listed under the categories of

- Special education.
- Related services.
- Supplementary services and aids.
- Program modifications or supports for school personnel.

This chapter will define each of these terms and give examples of what they mean. Services and supports are provided to help students to

- Advance appropriately toward attaining the annual goals.
- Be involved and progress in the general curriculum.
- Participate in extracurricular and other nonacademic activities.
- Learn and interact with the student population as a whole.

The special education and services that will be provided for a student should flow directly from the student's goals and objectives. That is, if Stephen's goal this year is to move from a sign language vocabulary of 25 words to a vocabulary of 50 words, what support and services will he need? The more specific and measurable the goals are, the easier it will be to figure out what level, intensity, and duration of services are needed.

If you have never helped to design a special education program for a student, you might find it helpful to review the way that "special education" is defined by IDEA.

Special education means:

- *Specially designed instruction*, at no cost to the parents, to meet a student's unique needs. Adaptations are made in the *content* or *delivery* of instruction so that the student can access the general education curriculum and meet the standards set for all students in that location. The instruction itself may be provided in a variety of settings, such as the school, home, in hospitals or institutions, or in other settings. Instruction in physical education is specifically included here (see Chapter 10).

▸ A service, such as speech pathology, if it is "specially designed instruction" and considered as special education under your state laws.

▸ Vocational education, if it is "instruction."

▸ "At no cost" means that all specially designed instruction is provided without charge, but this does not preclude incidental fees that are normally charged to nondisabled students as a part of the general education program.

One more thing to note about the definition of special education:

▸ A student is not defined as having a disability unless the student needs special education.

▸ Related services are provided to help a student to benefit from special education.

▸ Therefore, if a student does not need special education, the student is not eligible to receive "related services." (See the following discussion for a description of "related services.")

As your IEP team designs a student's special education program, you will need to consider whether accommodations or modifications are needed in content or instruction. Which parts of the general education curriculum can the student access with accommodations? Which parts, if any, need modification in content?

Your team will also need to consider whether the student needs related services. "Related services" are provided to help a student benefit from special education. They are defined as meaning transportation, and developmental, corrective, and supportive services that are required to assist a student with a disability to benefit from special education, including

▸ Speech-language pathology and audiology services.

▸ Psychological services.

▸ Physical and occupational therapy.

▸ Recreation, including therapeutic recreation.

▸ Early identification and assessment of disabilities in preschool children.

▸ Counseling services, including rehabilitation counseling.

▸ Orientation and mobility services.

▸ Medical services for diagnostic and evaluation purposes.

▸ School health services.

▸ Social work services in schools.

▸ Parent counseling and training.

This list is not meant to be exhaustive. Other supportive services could include artistic and cultural programs, art, music, and dance therapy, travel training, and nutrition services.

Today, many of these special services are provided in general classrooms. The specialist may either work with one student or with a group of students (with and without disabilities) in the classroom or may instruct the classroom teacher or aide so that they can deliver the service. For example, an occupational or physical therapist may bring adaptive equipment into the classroom either to work directly on specific motor skills or to provide a physical accommodation so that the student can complete a task. At other times, the related service provider may opt to pull the child from a classroom on a regular basis to provide special services. With computerized assistive devices such as large screen print, Braille writers, and computerized speech, students are able to complete more school tasks and function more independently.

Let's look at the list of "related services" one by one:

Speech-Language Pathology and Audiology Services

Audiology services, which are often provided by audiologists, can

- Identify students who have hearing losses.
- Determine the range, nature, and degree of the loss, and provide a referral for medical or other professional help, if necessary.
- Provide instruction in areas such as language improvement or lipreading.
- Determine a student's need for group or individual voice amplification, select and fit a hearing aid, and evaluate the effectiveness of amplification.

Speech-language pathology services include

- The identification, diagnosis, and appraisal of specific speech or language impairments.
- Referral for medical or other necessary professional attention for improving speech or language impairments.
- Providing services to help improve or prevent communicative impairments.
- Counseling and guidance for parents, students, and teachers regarding speech and language impairments.

Psychological Services

The school psychologist can

- Administer psychological and educational tests and other assessments to the student.
- Interpret assessment results.
- Obtain, integrate, and interpret information about the student's behavior and conditions as these relate to learning.
- Consult with staff members to plan school programs that will meet a student's special needs.

- Plan and manage a program of psychological services, including counseling for students and their families.
- Assist with designing positive behavior intervention strategies for students whose behavior is disruptive to others.

Physical and Occupational Therapy

Qualified physical therapists can help students with gross motor skills and development. They might help students with sitting, standing, walking, or posture. Physical therapists also work with students whose bodies are rigid because of cerebral palsy or other disabilities, and they can help students with orthopedic impairments improve function. Occupational therapists focus on fine motor skills that are needed to improve a student's independent functioning at home, in the classroom, and in nonacademic activities such as physical education, electives, or recess.

Recreation, Including Therapeutic Recreation

These services would be provided to

- Assess a student's leisure or play skills.
- Provide therapeutic services, if necessary.
- Support recreation programs in schools and community agencies.
- Provide education about how to spend one's leisure time.

Early Identification And Assessment of Disabilities in Preschool Children

This term means the adoption and carrying out of a formal plan to identify a disability as early as possible in a child's life. See Chapter 11 for more information.

Counseling Services, Including Rehabilitation Counseling

Counseling services are provided by qualified social workers, psychologists, guidance counselors, or other qualified personnel. Rehabilitation counseling can be given in individual or group sessions, and it focuses on career development, employment preparation, achieving independence, and integration in the workplace and community.

Orientation and Mobility Services

"Orientation and mobility services" was added to the list of examples of related services in 1997. These are services for blind or visually impaired students to help them to become oriented to and move safely around their homes, schools, and communities. This can include

- ▸ Teaching spatial and environmental concepts, as well as how to use sensory information (such as sound, temperature, and vibrations) to travel (for example, using sound at a traffic light to cross the street).
- ▸ Teaching students to use the long cane to travel safely through an environment.
- ▸ Teaching students to use remaining vision and distance low-vision aids, as appropriate.

Other skills may be taught as well, including but not limited to

- ▸ Awareness of body position, movements, and direction.
- ▸ How to protect one's body by using basic skills such as arm and hand protective techniques.
- ▸ Community street crossings and use of accessible pedestrian signs.
- ▸ Independent travel within the community, including the use of public transportation systems such as fixed route bus systems, subways, and commuter trains.
- ▸ Use of community resources available to people who are blind or visually impaired to assist with safe and efficient community travel.

Medical Services for Diagnostic and Evaluation Purposes

Medical services are provided by licensed physicians to determine if a student's disability results in a need for special education and related services. These are diagnostic services and do not cover other medical needs such as immunizations, surgery, or routine office checkups.

School Health Services

Students with disabilities may have need of specialized health services. Most schools have arrangements for a nurse or other qualified professional to be available to assist with dispensing medications and performing a variety of other nursing tasks consistent with your state's nurse practice act. The school nurse or other professional makes decisions regarding the delegation of nursing tasks and provides ongoing training and direction to assistive personnel. To dispense medication at school, an information sheet on the medication and dosage must be signed by the prescribing physician and returned to the school.

Today, medication is often prescribed for students who have been diagnosed as having an "attention deficit hyperactivity disorder" (ADHD), although other options such as behavioral contracting and reduction of extraneous environmental stimuli may also be effective. In general, teachers try to use other procedures before turning to medications such as Ritalin. Diagnosis of ADHD is a medical decision and the diagnosis must be made by a physician (although there are standardized psychological tests that will provide indicators of ADHD). If a child receives a medical diagnosis of ADHD and medication is required during the school day, both dosage and timing of the dosage will be very important. Teachers will need to coordinate this carefully with parents and physicians.

In schools serving special populations such as children with fragile medical conditions or physical disabilities, a school nurse may be present at all times and may assist with monitoring various medical conditions, as well as handling emergency situations.

Social Work Services in Schools

Social work services include

- ‣ Preparing a social or developmental history for a student with a disability.
- ‣ Providing group or individual counseling for the student and family.
- ‣ Working with problems in a student's living situation (at home, at school, or in the community) that affect the student's adjustment to school.
- ‣ Mobilizing school and community resources to help the student learn as effectively as possible.
- ‣ Helping to develop positive behavioral intervention strategies for students whose behavior is disruptive to themselves or others.

Parent Counseling and Training

These services are intended to help parents to understand the special needs of their children, as well as provide them with information about child development.

Transportation

Students with disabilities may need instruction in traveling around their school, or to and from school. A high school student with a mental disability, for example, might need to be taught how to get from class to class. Training in safe traveling among homes, schools, and the community can be provided for any student for whom this is an issue.

Transportation services assist the student with disabilities, other than students who have visual impairments, with travel training, including but not limited to:

- ‣ Travel to and from school.
- ‣ Travel in and around school buildings.
- ‣ Travel between schools.
- ‣ Special equipment if necessary, such as special or adapted buses, ramps, and lifts.

Most students with disabilities will receive the same transportation services as other students traveling to that school. Integrated transportation can be accomplished with lifts and other equipment on regular school transportation vehicles.

Now that we have considered related services, we will move on to consider another category of assistance called "supplementary aids and services." Supplementary aids and services means aids, services, and other supports that are provided in general education classes or other education-related settings to enable students with disabilities to be educated with nondisabled students to the maximum extent appropriate. The focus here is on education in the general education classroom, and the provision of necessary aids and services to make that education program appropriate and effective.

Whereas related services are provided to help a student benefit from *special education*, supplementary aids and services are provided to help a student benefit from *general education classes*. Supplementary aids and services should focus on components such as necessary accommodations, instructional and assistive technology, materials and equipment, and the use of paraprofessionals and assistants — all supporting the work in the general education classroom of the special and general education teachers and the related services specialists.

Another kind of support for students with disabilities is known as "program modifications or supports for school personnel." These would typically include the following:

- Time for planning, problem-solving, and collaboration for special and general education teachers.
- The provision of paraprofessionals and assistants.
- Inservice training for special and general education teachers and other involved professionals.
- The elimination of unnecessary paperwork for teachers.
- The provision of supports through technology, personnel, and management reforms aimed at substantially limiting the still-necessary paperwork obligation for teachers.

This chapter has examined the special education, services, and supports that can help students with disabilities to participate in the general education curriculum and classrooms. Entwined with these issues is the decision about where the student receives his educational program and services, which we will discuss in the following chapter.

Chapter 8
A Free Appropriate Public Education,
the Least Restrictive Environment,
and Time and Duration of Services

As the IEP team considers the special education and services that a student needs, it must also consider where these services will be best provided. This is commonly referred to as a "placement" decision.

As we have explained previously, IDEA '97 affirms the following principles:

- That students with disabilities are first and foremost part of the general school community.
- That students with disabilities should (as should all students) be held to higher educational standards and be working within the general education classroom, when appropriate, on the general education curriculum as the first placement option. If that can't work, even with special supports and services, then the student receives services outside of the general education classroom. Many students with disabilities receive services in both settings.

A common misperception is that providing the same general education curriculum to all students means complete inclusion in the general education classroom. But the "general education curriculum" is *not* a place. It can be effectively provided in other settings when appropriate. Still, IDEA '97 reemphasizes the importance of starting with the general education classroom as the first placement option and trying to make this placement work.

Placement decisions are made as you consider, weigh, and balance two critical factors:

- Providing a free and appropriate education program.
- In the least restrictive environment.

A "free appropriate public education" (or FAPE) refers to special education and related services that

- Are provided at public expense, under public supervision and direction, and without charge.

- ▸ Meet your state's standards.
- ▸ Include preschool, elementary school, or secondary school education.
- ▸ Are provided in conformity with an IEP that meets the requirements of law.

The "least restrictive environment" means that:

- ▸ Students with disabilities, including students in public or private institutions or other care facilities, are educated with students who are nondisabled to the maximum extent appropriate.
- ▸ Special classes, separate schooling, or other removal of students with disabilities from the general educational environment occurs only if the nature or severity of the disability is such that education in general classes with the use of supplementary aids and services cannot be achieved satisfactorily.

The IEP team considers a "continuum of alternative placements" including

- ▸ Instruction in general education classes, special classes, special schools, home instruction, and instruction in hospitals and institutions.
- ▸ A provision for supplementary services, such as a resource room or itinerant instruction, to be provided in conjunction with general education class placement.

The team must determine the least restrictive setting in which to deliver the services. Generally instruction can be delivered in the general education classroom with some level of supplementary aids and/or services. Some students may require individual or small group instruction which may be delivered within the general classroom setting, or a special class or learning center setting.

The student's placement must be

- ▸ Determined at least annually.
- ▸ Based on the student's IEP.
- ▸ As close as possible to the student's home.

The overriding rule is that placement decisions must be made on an individual basis, student by student, subject by subject, and not unilaterally. Unless a student's IEP requires some other arrangement, the student is educated in the school and classroom that he would attend if he were not disabled. And in selecting the least restrictive environment, consideration must be given to any potential harmful effect on the student or on the quality of services that he needs.

Students with disabilities must also be provided with *nonacademic* services in as integrated a setting as possible. This is especially important for students who spend their school days exclusively with other students with disabilities. The IEP team needs to look at student participation in a range of services and activities, including meals, recess periods, athletics and recreational activities, school clubs, school employment, school assistance with employment, and counseling and health services.

The following discussion guidelines may be useful in determining the most appropriate and least restrictive setting in which services are to be provided:

- In what areas is the student successful? If he is successful in these areas, why remove the student from the general education environment?
- In what areas is the student experiencing difficulty? Have modifications or accommodations been tried? What will it take to keep the student in the general education environment? Discuss supplementary aids and services, and modifications (including Braille or assistive technology) that would be needed for the student to succeed in various educational settings.
- Discuss where special education services have been provided, where the student now receives services, and what supports and services are presently recommended to meet the student's needs. Discuss the sites and settings that were considered previously and describe why they were not chosen.
- If, for any given subject area, it appears that the student will not learn successfully in the general education environment, even with the use of supplementary aids and services, what is the appropriate environment? How can we deliver services to the student so that the student can achieve his goals?
- How much time will the student interact with his nondisabled peers? What opportunities can we make available for the student to interact with his nondisabled peers, if he needs to be removed for any amount of time from the general education environment?

Placement decisions are usually (but not always) made by the IEP team, but parents must always be members of any group that makes any significant decision about the educational placement of their child. You need to notify parents when even a relatively small change in placement seems desirable. For example, suppose that David listens to books on tape in the general education classroom, and his parents strongly support inclusion. But as more students are assigned to David's classroom, the classroom gets noisier and harder to handle, so David's teacher decides that he should listen to the books on tape in the library. In this instance, because of their beliefs and priorities, David's parents should be notified about this placement change.

Finally the IEP for students with disabilities must include

- A statement of the special education, related services, supplementary aids, and services to be provided for the student, as well as any program modifications or supports for school personnel (as described in the preceding chapter).
- And also the projected date for the beginning of these services and modifications, as well as their anticipated frequency, location, and duration.

This means that the IEP must be clear about

- ▸ When the services will begin (for example, on September 1st or the first day of school).
- ▸ How often the services will be delivered (for example, three times a week for an hour).
- ▸ The location (the general classroom or a resource room, for example).
- ▸ The duration of the services (3 months? 6 months? the entire school year?).

The amount and level of services to be committed must be appropriate and clearly stated on the IEP.

In this chapter we have considered placement decisions and concepts such as a "free appropriate public education" and the "least restrictive environment." In the next chapter, we will take on the issues of the evaluation of students with disabilities and the students' participation in state- and local-level general education assessments.

Chapter 9
Evaluation and Assessment

This chapter will consider two issues:

▸ Participation of students with disabilities in state- and local-level assessments of student achievement.
▸ Evaluations to determine whether students are meeting their IEP goals, objectives, and benchmarks.

Participation of Students with Disabilities in State- and Local-Level Assessments of Student Achievement

As we have previously discussed in Chapter 1, the IEP now must describe any "individual modifications" in the administration of state- or district-wide assessments of student achievement that are needed in order for a student with a disability to participate. If the IEP team decides that a student will not participate in a particular state- or district-wide assessment (or part of an assessment), then the team must explain why the assessment is not appropriate for the student and how the student will be assessed.

In Chapter 1 we explained how difficult it has been to determine how students with disabilities have scored on state- and district-level general education assessments. We do know that many students have been excluded from these tests. Reasons for this include the following:

▸ Adults want to protect students from the stress of taking rigorous tests.
▸ There are pressures to exclude students in states and districts with "high stakes" accountability systems. In some states, the consequences for districts and schools whose students score poorly on state tests are serious. As a result, there can be a tendency for schools to exclude students who, it is thought, will score poorly on state tests.
▸ The guidelines for the participation of students with disabilities in such assessments vary widely and are carried out differently at the local level.
▸ There is inadequate monitoring to see if and how these guidelines are followed.

Why include students with disabilities in state- and district-level tests of student achievement?

- To promote high expectations for the achievement of students with disabilities and to make sure they are making progress.
- To obtain an accurate picture of student achievement nationwide. This can't be done if a significant percentage of students are excluded.
- To allow school districts to be compared fairly to one another. This can't be done if one district includes all students in its assessments, while another district excludes large numbers of students.
- To make sure that students with disabilities are included in other elements of general education reform. Unless some educators know that students with disabilities will be included in state tests, they might not take seriously the responsibility to include those students in other general education reforms of teaching and learning.
- To avoid unintended consequences of "high stakes" accountability systems. As was said above, these accountability systems can lead to a tendency for schools to exclude students who, it is thought, will score poorly on state tests. Also, other nondisabled students who might score poorly might be retained in grade or referred to special education to avoid low scores for the school.
- To meet the new requirements of IDEA '97.

Including students with disabilities in state and local assessments provides big challenges, given their lack of participation to date. But it is important to understand that there are big opportunities, too, in terms of bringing students with disabilities more firmly into the general education system.

Start with the assumption that all students will participate in state or local assessments in one of three ways:

- With no accommodations.
- With accommodations (such as untimed tests, adapted formats, oral and taped responses, or reading the instructions orally). Increasingly, states are developing lists of approved accommodations for testing.
- Through an alternative assessment for the small number of students for whom the state- or district-level test is clearly inappropriate.

Don't start by assuming that every student with disabilities needs accommodations for state- or district-wide general education assessments:

- Start with the assumption that all students will participate in general education assessments if they are learning the content, no matter where the instruction occurs.
- Remember that all students will participate in some way. The IEP team is responsible for making the final decisions about these assessments, although these decisions must follow state laws.
- Make decisions based on the student's level of functioning and learning characteristics, not on the program setting, category of disability, or percentage of

time in the general education classroom. The decision is based on the unique learning needs of each individual student.

Remember that accommodations in test taking

- Are provided to meet student needs, not to give anyone an advantage.
- Allow a student to demonstrate what the student knows and can do.
- Won't eliminate frustration for the student.
- Won't guarantee a good score for the student.

In making decisions about accommodations:

- Accommodations used in assessments should parallel accommodations used in instruction. A student shouldn't encounter an accommodation for the first time during an assessment.
- Make decisions about accommodations based on the way that the student accesses instruction, not on the student's disability or placement.
- The decision should be made by the parents and the team and noted on the IEP or on a form attached to the IEP.

Accommodations usually fit into four categories:

- *Setting*. Where is the test administered? In a small group or individually? With adaptive furniture or special acoustics? Would the student's accommodation distract other test takers?
- *Presentation or format of the test*. Does the student need large print or oral directions, for example?
- *Timing or scheduling*. Should the test be broken down into subtasks? In what order? Is a longer time period needed to complete the test?
- *Response mode*. Can the student write or does she need a computer to respond, for example? Some students may not "fill in the circles" on multiple choice exams, but indicate their answer on the test form in another way. This can be transcribed later.

You may decide, for a small percentage of students with serious disabilities, that state- or district-wide assessments are a clearly inappropriate way for the student to demonstrate what he knows and can do. In this case, you can consider alternative assessments. Alternative assessments have not been widely available to date, but this will change. By July 1, 2000, all states must have developed and must begin using alternative assessments. Until this time, teachers may have to design individual alternative assessments that could include portfolios, observations, and demonstrations of performance.

Evaluations to Determine Whether Students Are Meeting Their IEP Goals, Objectives, and Benchmarks

The IEP must include a description of how the student's progress toward his annual goals will be measured. You must also describe how the parents will be regularly informed (by such means as periodic report cards, and at least as often as parents are informed of their nondisabled students' progress) of

▸   The student's progress toward meeting the annual goals.

▸   The extent to which that progress is sufficient to enable the student to achieve the goals by the end of the year.

Assessments and evaluations of student progress should be understandable and clearly linked to benchmarks or short-term objectives. Tied to each benchmark or objective should be:

▸   *Procedures for reviewing progress*:
       How will we measure progress? With which charts or assessments?
       Who will be responsible for monitoring the measurement?
       Can evaluation results be demonstrated (e.g., charts, work samples, test scores)?
       Has student performance been observed?

▸   *Criteria for determining success or failure*:
       What do we expect the student to do? How many times? At what level?
       What will we accept as success or mastery of the objective?
       Are the criteria directly linked to the present levels of educational performance?

▸   *A schedule for reviewing progress*:
       Is it necessary to review the student's progress more often than for students without disabilities? If yes, then when will we review each objective? Will we review in one week? One month? Nine weeks? If the objectives are truly the intermediate steps to reach the goal, then the schedule for review should look at each step. Will we need to meet if the student is not accomplishing her objectives?

You also need to consider

▸   Who will be responsible for evaluating the student's ongoing progress toward accomplishing the objective?

▸   Where will the evaluation be conducted? Where will we expect the student to accomplish the objectives? In one environment or multiple environments? In class? At home? In the community?

Now that we have covered the issues of assessments and evaluations, we will look, in the next chapter, at a number of special factors that the IEP team needs to consider, as well as services provided through physical education and an extended school year.

Chapter 10
Special Factors
(Behavior, Diversity, Braille, Communication Needs, and Assistive Technology), Physical Education, and the Extended School Year

IDEA '97 requires that the IEP team consider "special factors" if they are applicable to a particular student with disabilities. We will discuss these special factors in this chapter, as well as requirements for all students with disabilities related to physical education and an extended school year.

Special factors are, in many instances, common sense issues that IEP teams have often considered. But with the creation of IDEA '97, there was a concern that these issues were not always considered uniformly nationwide. Now, your team must document that you looked at these issues, if necessary:

▸ Strategies, including positive behavioral interventions and supports, for students whose behavior impedes their own learning or other students' learning.
▸ The language needs of students with limited English proficiency, as these needs relate to the student's IEP.
▸ Instruction in Braille and the use of Braille for students who are blind or visually impaired, unless the IEP team determines that such instruction is not appropriate for a student.
▸ Students' communication needs, particularly for students who are deaf or hard of hearing.
▸ The need for assistive technology devices and services.

We will now look at these special factors one by one.

Behavior and Discipline

We will cover three general topics under this section on behavior and discipline:

▸ Positive behavioral interventions, as required for students whose behavior impedes the learning of self or others.
▸ A sample crisis management plan for a seriously dangerous incident.
▸ IDEA '97's requirements regarding discipline, suspension, and expulsion.

As was stated above, IDEA '97 directs IEP teams to consider positive behavioral interventions, strategies, and supports for students whose behavior impedes the learning of self or others. These students may be interrupting classrooms with behavior such as making noise, yelling, pacing, or throwing books. They may also engage in behaviors that are hurtful to themselves or others. Behaviors such as these must obviously be handled for any student, whether they have disabilities or not.

Behavior management plans should use, as their reference, the standard conduct and behavior that is expected of all students at school and in the community. The district discipline code, for example, might be your source for describing standard conduct. When developing the behavior management plan, the IEP team should carefully listen to perspectives and thoughts of all of its members, including the student, the family, and general and special educators. The IEP team should also consider whether any of the student's other teachers should be contacted and invited to provide comments or to participate in the development of this plan.

In order to develop a behavior management plan, the IEP team needs to arrange for a "functional behavioral assessment" for the student. These assessments use a variety of strategies to investigate the causes of unacceptable behavior and to suggest what kinds of interventions might work. For example, a student who throws a book may be expressing frustration, a desire for attention or power, boredom, or anger. A deeper understanding of the behavior can help the IEP team to design appropriate interventions.

The IEP team should consider which positive behavior interventions will help students function in the classroom without interfering with other students' learning. The prevention of behavior problems should be creative and focused on the student's strengths, interests, and needs. The team may want to consider and experiment with creative and constructive plans such as community service, in-school services, and volunteering to clean, tutor, work on the landscape, or do office work. The purpose is to prevent and avoid more severe and damaging disciplinary actions such as suspensions.

After the positive behavior intervention plan has been developed, the IEP team should let the student's teachers know about the plan and their roles in carrying it out. Teachers need to know what their responsibilities are, and IEP team members need to consider whether teachers will need training or other support to carry out their roles. Your IEP team should also know that it's okay if they aren't sure if a behavior management plan will work. Sometimes the team must experiment with an approach, knowing that the strategy can be changed if it doesn't work. The important thing is to give a potential solution a fair opportunity to work.

There are many good systems for promoting good behavior. Strategies exist that are school-wide, classroom-wide, and specific to an individual. This important issue is bigger than we can cover in this book, but in Appendix II you will find additional resources about positive behavior management strategies and functional behavioral assessment.

The IEP team might consider the following kinds of questions in figuring out whether a behavior component should be incorporated into the IEP:

- ▸ Has the IEP team determined behavior to be an issue?
- ▸ Does the student demonstrate behaviors that are unsafe to himself or others, or that significantly interfere with the learning environment?
- ▸ Were previous behavioral interventions attempted?
- ▸ Is the student's behavior related to, or a manifestation of, a disability? Is the problem behavior linked to a skill deficit?
- ▸ Does the student have the skill, but, for some reason, not the desire to modify his behavior?
- ▸ Does the student's special instruction include the use of techniques that may be considered intrusive (such as time-out, or withdrawal of reinforcement or privileges)?
- ▸ Has the student been removed from the general education classroom for an excessive amount of time because of his behavior?

If the team answers "yes" to any of these questions, you will want to consider incorporating a new behavior component into the IEP or into an IEP amendment, or develop a new IEP. In doing this, you can consider adding elements to the following parts of the IEP:

Present Levels of Performance
- ▸ Has the behavior(s) of concern been defined in observable, measurable terms?
- ▸ Have the frequency and intensity of the behavior been identified to establish a baseline for educational planning?

Annual Goals
- ▸ Are goals written that indicate what a student can be expected to accomplish in one year to reduce or eliminate the behavior?
- ▸ Are the goals written to describe new skills a student can be expected to demonstrate in one year?

Benchmarks or Objectives
- ▸ Are sequential steps developed for each goal? That is, has the team identified what can reasonably be accomplished at various intervals, such as report card periods?
- ▸ Are criteria and evaluation procedures included for each objective?

What if There Is a Crisis Involving Behavior?

Schools may need to develop emergency response plans for the classroom in case there is ever a crisis regarding behavior. Ohio's *Rules for the Education of Handicapped Children* encourages school districts to have a crisis intervention plan — or if school districts don't have a plan, then they are required to employ at least one full-time aide in every class for students with serious emotional disturbances.

The plan should

▸ Include the name of the teacher and of the administrator who is responsible for the plan.

▸ Specify who (such as a psychologist or supervisor) will help the teacher with advice, suggestions, counseling, and other assistance.

▸ Identify who will help to intervene during a crisis. This could be a principal, secretary, custodian, or anyone who is in the building and does not have the direct responsibility for teaching students at the time that they are to be available. If there are multiple classrooms, then there must be a plan in case more than one classroom needs help at the same time. Specific policies and plans must be adopted to describe the training for a person who is assigned to intervene.

▸ Describe what the person who is assigned to intervene in a crisis is supposed to do. How is this person notified about a crisis? What steps are followed to bring the situation under control? What does the teacher do?

▸ Be provided to everyone involved, reviewed at least annually, and evaluated in writing.

Other Considerations

▸ Are suggested support services and resources identified to support the plan (such as aide services, behavior specialists, counseling, social skills materials, or professional development activities)?

▸ For intervention techniques considered to be intrusive or that have the potential for being abused (such as time-out or passive restraint), are procedures for their use identified and are the circumstances under which they will be used described?

▸ Are the behavior interventions guided by principles of professional best practice?

▸ Are there procedures for notifying the parent when intervention has been necessary?

▸ Is there a review process or schedule established?

▸ Is there a process for assessing the effectiveness of the behavior plan?

Now we have looked at the issues of behavior management and crisis planning, we will turn briefly to the issues of discipline and suspension. In general, a student may be disciplined according to general school guidelines unless there is a change in the student's placement. The most common changes in placement resulting from discipline are an accumulation of more than 10 days of suspension in one school year, or if the student has been placed in an alternative educational setting for more than 10 days. The requirements regarding the suspension of students with disabilities are complex, meaning that you must consult your own state and local guidelines if you need specific assistance with this issue.

In general

▸   A student with a disability may be suspended from school (if need be) according to general school policies if the student is suspended for a total of 10 days or fewer in one school year. This length of suspension (10 days or fewer) is not considered a change in placement. The school is *not* required to provide special education services to a student during a suspension *if* the days of suspension total 10 days or fewer in one school year.

▸   States must make a free and appropriate education available to students with disabilities who have been suspended or expelled from school for more than 10 days in one school year. The student must receive the general education curriculum, physical education, services to help the student achieve his IEP goals, and services to address his behavior problem.

▸   School personnel may move a student with disabilities to an interim alternative education setting for up to 45 days, if the student has brought a weapon to school or a school function, or if the student knowingly possesses or uses illegal drugs, or sells or solicits the sale of a controlled substance while at school or a school function.

▸   Schools may ask a hearing officer to move a student with disabilities to an interim alternative education setting for up to 45 days, if the school believes that a student is substantially likely to injure himself or others in current placement. The hearing officer must consider whether the evidence of injury is "substantial," whether the student's current placement is appropriate, and whether the school has made reasonable efforts to minimize the risk of harm, including the use of supplementary aids and services.

▸   Parents must be part of the decision-making process regarding any change in placement. For example, if the school decides to change a student's placement for more than 10 days, the parents must be notified *on the day the decision was made* and informed of all procedural safeguards that apply. Schools have a number of other requirements in regard to parents, so it is essential that you consult your school district if any change in placement is being contemplated.

▸   If a student with disabilities is suspended, the school district must find out if it has previously conducted a functional behavior assessment of the student and carried out a behavior management plan. If these things have not been done, then the IEP team must meet to develop an assessment plan and appropriate behavioral interventions to address the problematic behavior. If the student already has a behavior management plan, then the IEP team must review the plan and modify it, as necessary, to address the problem. These actions are required *unless* the suspension is for 10 days or fewer and no further disciplinary action is contemplated.

▸ If a school decides to suspend a student with disabilities, the IEP team must meet within ten days to determine whether the misconduct was a "manifestation" of the student's disability. The results of this inquiry will determine what kind of discipline options are available for the student. Again, this action is required *unless* the suspension is for 10 days or fewer and no further disciplinary action is contemplated.

For more information on this and other topics related to discipline and suspension, consult your local experts. We emphasize that the laws covering suspension and expulsion are complex, containing protections for the school, families, and students. What we have provided here is a brief summary. You must check out your own state laws and district policies and get assistance from your school district if you need any help with the issues of punishment, suspension, or expulsion.

Linguistic and Cultural Diversity, and English as a Second Language

In developing an IEP for a student with limited English proficiency (LEP), the IEP team must consider how the student's level of English language proficiency affects the special education and related services that the student needs. Under the Civil Rights Act of 1964, school districts are required to provide LEP students with alternative language services so that students can become proficient in English and participate in all available educational programs, including special education. A LEP student with a disability may require special services to develop her English language skills, as well as to complete other aspects of her educational program. For a LEP student with a disability, the IEP must address whether the special education and related services that the student needs will be provided in a language other than English.

The IEP team also needs to look at the question of cultural diversity, as appropriate. Consider that by the year 2000, nearly one in three Americans will be either African American, Hispanic, Asian American, or Native American. And taken together as a group, "minority" students are comprising an ever larger percentage of public school students. Large city school populations are overwhelmingly "minority."

IDEA '97 is not specific in describing what the IEP team should do regarding the issue of diversity, beyond the requirements stated above. However, here are some factors that you might want to consider:

▸ It can be difficult to separate a student's lack of proficiency in English from a learning disability. Information from a variety of sources, formal and informal, from the home and school, looking at the student's mastery of her native language as well as English, will help the team to determine whether this is a disability or a linguistic difference. Someone with expertise associated with linguistic diversity should be added, if possible, to the IEP team. This person can help determine, for example, whether a student's English skills are developed to the point where the student can fully function in an English-only program — and separate any problems the student is having in this regard from the presence of a disability. Remember that someone who is bilingual and of the same culture does not necessarily have expertise in analyzing data and discerning its implications for planning.

▸ Bearing the dual labels of "disability" and "linguistic difference" is difficult for students. But don't reduce your expectations for these students' achievement. Stress higher-level skills at the same time as you teach them basic skills. Students with limited English proficiency and a disability will need special instruction that melds the best instructional practices from both fields. In a general education classroom, it will be important to carefully monitor new vocabulary and introduce new vocabulary with concrete examples. Language development for these students should be embedded into all classroom subjects. Even if a student cannot handle the reading requirements for particular subjects, she may be able to participate in class discussions.

▸ Sometimes when a student receives special education services, English-as-a-Second-Language and bilingual services are stopped. Remember that students have a right to all of these services. This will require coordination among service providers, since there can be many transitions as a student moves from program to program, and her progress needs to be tracked. There are great challenges for a student in becoming well-integrated into the school and general education curriculum when the student has both disabilities and language and cultural differences.

▸ Written notes, letters, and information that are given to parents must be in their native language, unless this is clearly not feasible.

▸ Think about how to work more closely with parents. Consider that more time and effort may be needed to establish a trusting relationship with people of different cultural backgrounds. You will need an interpreter in some instances. Be aware of your own biases regarding other cultures, but don't let it bias your judgment of a student. Respect a student's differences and her native culture, but also be aware that the student must learn how to fit into the larger school community.

▸ In regard to assessments, English language learners must be held to the same high standards as other students. You may have to think about how to involve them in state and district assessments when they also have a disability. How, for example, can students make the transition from assessments in their native language to full participation in general assessments?

Braille

In the case of a student who is blind or visually impaired, the IEP team must provide for instruction in Braille and the use of Braille unless the team determines that this is not appropriate. To do this, they must evaluate

- The student's reading and writing skills.
- The student's needs.
- Appropriate reading and writing media for the student.
- An evaluation of the student's future needs for instruction in Braille or the use of Braille.

IDEA '97 specifically requires that Braille be considered for students with severe vision limitations. There was a concern that Braille is not always considered for these students.

Your IEP team may want to consider:

- Was a print or Braille assessment made?
- Was Braille instruction considered?
- Was literature describing the benefits of Braille instruction reviewed by those developing the IEP?
- Were one or more reading and writing media in which instruction is appropriate specified on the IEP?
- How will the use of Braille reading and writing be integrated into a student's entire curriculum when Braille is specified as an appropriate medium for the student?
- How will a student's reading and writing skills be assessed in each medium?

Communication Needs

In the case of a student who has trouble communicating or is deaf or hard of hearing, the IEP team must consider the student's

- Language and communication needs.
- Opportunities for direct communications with peers and professionals in the student's language and communication mode.
- Academic level.
- Full range of needs, including opportunities for direct instruction in the student's language and communication model.

Notice that the team is required to consider opportunities for the student to *directly* communicate with peers and professionals.

Assistive Technology

The IEP should indicate whether a student needs assistive technology or services in order to meet her educational goals and access the general education curriculum. Assistive technology devices are items, pieces of equipment, or systems that can maintain or improve the functional capabilities of students with disabilities.

Technological devices can help with issues such as mobility, communication, hearing, or sight. Examples include wheelchairs, specially designed toilet seats, electronic communication devices, hearing aids, large print books, or special computer software.

Assistive technology *services* assist a student in selecting, acquiring, or using an assistive technology device. For example, services can help with

- Evaluating a student's need for technological assistance.
- Selecting, designing, purchasing, repairing, and maintaining equipment.
- Training and technical assistance for a student, family, or school professionals in using the technology.

The issue of assistive technology is complex and can not be covered in depth in this publication, but much useful information will be found in *Has Technology Been Considered? A Guide for IEP Teams* (see Appendix II). However, the developers of this guide have a few words of advice regarding students, assistive technology, and the IEP:

- The need for technology must be well-documented, with top priority given to technology that can help students with fundamental functions such as communication or mobility.
- When writing the IEP and talking about assistive technology, be positive. Explain clearly what the technology will help the student to accomplish.
- Recognize that some students have an absolute need for a piece of equipment such as a motorized wheelchair. At other times, a device such as a communication board may be used as an occasional support.
- Issues of funding for assistive technology are sensitive, since some equipment is very expensive. It may be useful, sometimes, to describe what kind of technology a student needs, rather than to specify a brand name and price. You must, however, figure out what is right in your own circumstances.
- IDEA '97 strengthens a requirement for interagency coordination in providing and paying for services related to special education. Work with your district's special education coordinator to understand how this works in your state and school district.

Physical Education

Physical education services, specially designed if necessary, must be made available to every student with a disability. In fact, the term "special education" is defined by the Congress to include physical education, which is to be provided as an integral part of the educational program of every student with a disability.

Students must have the opportunity to participate in the general physical education program available to nondisabled students unless

▸   The student is enrolled full-time in a separate facility. In this case, the student still must receive appropriate physical education services.

▸   The student needs specially designed physical education, as prescribed in the student's IEP.

Physical education is defined as the development of

▸   Physical and motor fitness.
▸   Fundamental motor skills and patterns.
▸   Skills in aquatics, dance, and individual and group games and sports (including intramural and lifetime sports).

The term "physical education" also includes special physical education, adapted physical education, movement education, and motor development. When adapted physical education is provided, the IEP should include a present level of performance, annual goal, and short-term objectives or benchmarks related to this.

Your IEP team may need to consider the following kinds of questions in designing an appropriate physical education program:

▸   Is assessment data available from a qualified physical educator?
▸   Can the student's needs be addressed within the general physical education class? If not, why not?
▸   Are alternative physical education services needed for this student?
▸   Do the student's goals and objectives in this area address the needs identified in the assessment?
▸   Will ongoing technical assistance be available from a qualified physical educator?

Extended School Year

IDEA requires that "extended school year services" be provided to students who need them. Most students with disabilities can obtain an appropriate education during the regular school year, but this is not always true. A student's skills may regress unacceptably over the summer vacation. For example, a student with serious disabilities who has learned how to walk during the school year may lose this skill over the summer months. It might take a lot of time, during the fall, for the student to regain the ability to walk again.

The determination of whether a student needs extended school year services must be made on an individual basis by the IEP team. Many times, summer services are an abbreviated form of regular school services. Not every student with a disability is entitled to, or must receive, extended school year services. Each state develops its own standards for determining when a student needs these services, so consult your own state's requirements. Still, your IEP team might consider questions such as these if a student is failing to meet his goals and objectives:

- Are this student's goals and objectives reasonable and attainable in 1 year? What did we do when the student did not accomplish the first few objectives? Did we change the methodology? The technique? Did we conduct a review on schedule? Did we call for another meeting?
- Is the student likely to fail to achieve goals or objectives on his IEP due to an interruption of instruction during the summer? Will the student lose skills during the summer? Last fall, did the student take longer than was acceptable to "recapture" skills taught in the spring?
- Which extended services are needed during the summer? Are these the same as, or a portion of, the services provided during the regular school year? Will these services be provided by the school or by another agency? What will the student's summer program be?

In this chapter, we have discussed "special factors," physical education, and the extended school year. Next, we will look at services for young children with disabilities and the transition to preschool.

Chapter 11
Planning for Early Intervention, Preschool, and Kindergarten

Every state provides services for children with disabilities from the time they are born. In fact, all states provide services for IDEA-eligible students from birth through age 21. IDEA has three different programs depending on the age of the child: (1) Part C - Early Intervention (birth through age 2); (2) Part B, Section 619 - Preschool (for ages 3 to 5); and (3) Part B for school age children. The transitioning of children and families from one program to the next is an integral part of each program. Transition points include transition from early intervention to preschool; and from preschool to kindergarten and the school age IDEA provisions. The law provides two similar but discrete planning programs for young children. The youngest children aged birth through 2 have an Individualized Family Service Plan (IFSP). Children in preschool may continue with their IFSP under certain conditions or may have an IEP. School age children, including children in kindergarten, are served under an IEP.

While this chapter briefly addresses the IFSP, what is presented here is by no means a complete discussion, as this book is intended to focus on IEPs. We did feel it was important, however, to include a chapter on services for very young children and the programs that support them.

Early Intervention

As with special education for older students, there is an orderly cycle for determining whether a young child needs early intervention services. This cycle includes referral of the child from a parent or screening program, the assignment of a temporary services coordinator to work with the family, an evaluation of the child by a multidisciplinary team, and the determination of whether or not the child is eligible for services.

If the infant or toddler is found to be eligible for early intervention services, the family and a team of professionals meet to write an Individualized Family Service Plan (IFSP). The IFSP must be written down, conducted annually, and reviewed every 6 months. The IFSP team can, of course, meet more often if necessary. In any case, the IFSP must include

▸ Information about the child's level of physical, cognitive, communication, social, emotional, and adaptive development.

- A description of the family's resources, priorities, and concerns about supporting the development of their child.
- A description of the major outcomes that are expected for the child and family, along with timelines, as well as criteria and procedures for tracking progress.
- A description of the early intervention services that will be provided, including their frequency, the place where they will be delivered, and the way in which they will be delivered.
- A statement about the "natural environment" in which services will be delivered. A natural environment includes the home and other community settings where children without disabilities learn, play, and interact. If a child will not receive services in this kind of environment, then a justification must be provided.
- The date when services will start and the anticipated length of time that they will last.
- The identification of a "service coordinator" who is responsible for helping the family to carry out the IFSP and coordinate services for the family from various agencies.
- The steps that will be taken to support the transition of the toddler to a preschool or other appropriate services.

Transition from Early Intervention to Preschool

Local school districts are required to ensure that children participating in early intervention programs experience a smooth and effective transition to preschool. State systems to support early intervention programs for infants and toddlers with disabilities and their families were established in 1986. These services are intended to support the growth and development of children with disabilities from their earliest years, as well as to minimize their future need for special education. An essential part of this support is to strengthen the capacity of families to meet the special needs of their young children. Services are provided in a variety of settings at home and in the community, and include

- Family training, counseling, and home visits.
- Special instruction.
- Speech-language pathology and audiology services.
- Occupational therapy and physical therapy.
- Psychological services.
- Service coordination.
- Medical services only for diagnostic or evaluation purposes.
- Early identification, screening, and assessment services.
- Health services necessary to enable the infant or toddler to benefit from the other early intervention services.
- Social work services.
- Vision services.
- Assistive technology devices and assistive technology services.
- Transportation and related costs that are necessary to enable an infant or toddler and the family to receive a service described above.

States are required to have procedures to help toddlers and families negotiate the transition from early intervention programs to preschool. States must assure a smooth transition for toddlers by

- ▸ Making sure that the families of toddlers will be included in transition planning.
- ▸ Notifying local school districts that a toddler (who is receiving early intervention services) will soon reach the age of eligibility for preschool special education services.
- ▸ With family approval, convening a conference among the agency in charge of the early intervention services, the family, and the school district to discuss the special services that the child might need in preschool. This conference must be held at least 90 days (and if everyone agrees, up to 6 months) before the child is eligible for preschool services.
- ▸ Making reasonable efforts, with family approval, to convene a conference for a child who may not be eligible for special education services at preschool. The purpose of this conference is to discuss other services that the child might receive.
- ▸ Establishing procedures to review the child's program from the third birthday until the end of the school year.
- ▸ Establishing a transition plan for the child.

The requirements listed above were adopted to ease the transition to preschool for the family and the child. The transition for young children from early intervention services to preschool can be a big step. On one hand, it can be a time of pride as staff and parents think about the progress in the child's development and skills. On the other hand, teachers and service providers who have formed tight bonds with parents and children must start to disengage.

Preschool

Children enter preschool in one of two ways. They either transition from an early intervention program or they come in as new students who have been identified as a child with a disability. IDEA '97 has broadened the definition of a "child with a disability" to include, at state and local discretion, "a child aged three through nine who is experiencing developmental delays."

The definition of a child with a disability was expanded because it can be difficult to know the precise nature of a child's disability during the early years. The child may be struggling with one or more developmental tasks, from movement to talking or counting, but the reason may be unclear. "Use of 'developmental delay' as part of a unified approach will allow the special education and related services to be directly related to the child's needs and prevent locking the child into an eligibility category which may be inappropriate or incorrect, and could actually reduce later referrals of children with disabilities to special education" (*Senate Report*, IDEA '97).

A child in preschool may be directed by either an IFSP or an IEP. A child with a disability's right to a free and appropriate public education begins no later than the third birthday, and an IEP or IFSP must be in effect by that date. In the case of a child aged 3 through 5 (or at the discretion of the SEA, a 2-year-old child who turns 3 during the school year), an IFSP may serve as an IEP if

- This is consistent with state policy.
- It is agreed to by the agency providing services and the child's parents.
- The child's parents have been provided with a detailed explanation of the differences between an IFSP and an IEP.
- The child's parents choose the IFSP and they provide written informed consent.

At the preschool level, if an IFSP is being implemented to direct the child's activities, it must be congruent with age appropriate activities. In contrast, an IEP must be congruent with the general education curriculum.

Chapter 12
The Transition to Adult Life

Families, students, schools, and communities need to start thinking early about the adulthood of a student with a disability. Many serious questions need to be answered. For example, what will happen after high school graduation? Will the student be able to go to college? Move into a job? Leave home and live independently? Travel safely around the community, buy food, and handle money? What are the student's goals and what will it take to get there?

It can be tempting to put these questions off, particularly when students are young and everyone involved is busy and stressed enough without taking on anxieties about the future. But the future success of students with disabilities depends on early, effective, and cooperative planning by schools, community and private agencies, families, and students. This kind of planning addresses the important issues of where a young adult will live, work, relax, and develop friendships. It looks years into the future at the skills that the student will need, as well as at the supportive services that can be available once the student leaves school. This chapter will review some basic elements of transition planning, but for more in-depth information and many useful tips, consult The Council for Exceptional Children's publication *Integrating Transition Planning Into the IEP Process* (see Appendix II.)

In 1990, it was required that students with disabilities have "transition services" incorporated into their IEPs no later than age 16. IDEA '97 adds the additional requirement that a statement of the "transition service needs" of a student be part of the IEP *starting* at age 14. What do these requirements mean?

Transition services *needs* for 14- and 15-year-olds

▸   Focus on the student's course of study (such as participation in advanced-placement courses or a vocational education program).
▸   Look at how the student's curriculum addresses the knowledge and skills that the student will need after high school graduation.

Transition *services* starting at age 16 are a coordinated set of activities that

▸   Are designed within an outcome-oriented process that promotes movement from school to postschool activities, including postsecondary education, vocational training, integrated employment (including supported employment), continuing and adult education, adult services, independent living, or community participation.

- ▸ Are based on the individual student's needs, taking into account the student's preferences and interests.
- ▸ Include instruction, related services, community experiences, the development of employment and other postschool adult living objectives, acquisition of daily living skills and vocational evaluation, and other activities or services, as appropriate. If the IEP team determines that services are *not* needed in one or more of these areas, the IEP must include a statement to that effect and the basis upon which the determination was made.
- ▸ Include, if appropriate, a statement of the interagency responsibilities or any needed linkages with agencies.

Although transition needs must be considered for students starting at age 14, IEP teams can begin planning for the transition at any time — even in elementary school. Let's look briefly at the options listed in IDEA's requirements for a student with disabilities after high school graduation:

- ▸ *Postsecondary education* is one option, whether at junior or community colleges or at 4-year colleges or universities. Federal laws, including the Americans with Disabilities Act, prohibit discrimination against qualified students with disabilities in furthering their education.
- ▸ *Vocational training* at trade and technical schools prepare students for real-world jobs. The training may be of a short duration or may last several years. Students can also learn work skills through on-the-job training programs, internships, job shadowing, and job sampling. Some programs provide both an opportunity to learn and assistance with job placement afterwards.
- ▸ "*Integrated employment*" refers to a job where the young adult would be working with people who do not have disabilities. These could be jobs of any kind in the competitive labor market, full or part time. These jobs could also be "supported employment," which are basic skills jobs provided for workers with severe disabilities, usually at or near the minimum wage.
- ▸ *Continuing and adult education programs* provide a way to pursue personal interests or obtain job skills. Community colleges, universities, recreation departments, or local school districts may offer programs of this kind.
- ▸ *Adult service* programs provide a supervised setting for work and learning exclusively for adults with disabilities. For example, sheltered workshops may offer employment in contract work. Work activity centers may offer both training in personal living skills and in vocational skills. Adult day programs may help participants with day-to-day living, social, and recreational activities.
- ▸ *Independent living* for a person with disabilities is a goal that can be met in a number of settings. Depending on where he will live, the student needs to learn certain specific skills, such as handling money and transportation, shopping for food and other necessities, or managing his free time. The range of living options stretches from the home, an apartment, a supervised environment such as a group

home, to a special nursing home or intermediate care facility. It will take time and planning to choose where the student will live and to figure out what it will take to make that setting work.

- ► *Community participation* is another important item for the transition team to consider. How can the student continue to be a part of his community? Whether he attends church, volunteers to mow a neighbor's lawn, or joins a baseball team, the young adult will need opportunities to make friends and be active.

Transition planning starts with the student's needs, preferences, and interests. No one has a greater stake in the outcome! Throughout the planning process, students should be encouraged to speak out and give their opinions in whatever ways that this is possible. Transition planning is a good time for students to learn and practice, in a safe and supportive environment, how to express their thoughts in a way that makes others listen to them. This skill will be important as they move from the school into the community and into jobs and other living arrangements. There are also various prepackaged programs that can help students to identify their strengths, interests, and possible career paths. See Appendix II for resources on transition planning.

Your team will want to work with the student's family early in the transition process. How can they work through their hopes, thoughts, and concerns regarding the student? How can you help them with this process? *Negotiating the Special Education Maze* (listed in Appendix III) has a transition planning chart that families can use to organize their information, ideas, and priorities.

As with other parts of the IEP process, transition planning is a team effort. An important place to begin in assembling your team would be to find out if your school district has a transition coordinator. This person might have a variety of job titles, from "work study coordinator" to "case manager," but the job includes such tasks as making linkages among schools and public and private agencies, assessment and career counseling, transition planning, and program development and evaluation. The transition coordinator will know what kinds of resources and services your community has to support your student now and in the future, after he has left school. In addition, the school counselor may be able to assist with career awareness activities and identifying postsecondary options.

Who attends the transition meeting? The membership is the same as for the IEP team, except

- ► The student must be invited. If the student does not attend, then the IEP team must find other ways to make sure that the student's preferences and interests are considered.
- ► The school must invite a representative of any agency that is likely to be responsible for providing or paying for transition services. If the agencies don't send a representative, then the school must take other steps to obtain the participation of the agency in planning transition services.

Other attendees might include the student's vocational education instructor and representatives of community services such as a community college or mental health agency.

Starting at age 14 (or younger, if appropriate), invitations to the IEP team meeting must

- Indicate that a purpose of the meeting will be the development of a statement of the transition services needs of the student.
- Indicate that the school district will invite the student.

For a student with a disability beginning at age 16 (or younger) invitations must

- Indicate that a purpose of the meeting is the consideration of needed transition services for the student.
- Indicate that the school district will invite the student.
- Identify any other agencies that will be invited to send a representative.

Your team should select one team member to oversee and monitor the coordination of transition services. This person will be responsible for making sure that services are delivered and the transition plan is met. The student and family should feel comfortable about who this person is.

As with other parts of the IEP process, transition planning will require your team to consider and gather assessment data. Evaluation, of course, is an ongoing part of the IEP process, so your team will need to figure out what additional data it needs. For transition planning, you want to get a good idea about the student's strengths and suitability for various job or educational paths that the student and family are interested in exploring. Vocational assessments, for example, will help your team to understand the student's aptitudes and interests as they relate to possible career paths. These assessments can take many forms, from standardized testing, to observations inside and outside of school, observation checklists, and self- evaluation. The student, parents, teachers, job supervisors, and others all may offer different perspectives and information.

When the student is 14, the IEP team is required to look at ways in which a student's curriculum and course of study might be changed to support transition goals. The idea is to adapt or supplement the curriculum so that the student learns skills that are important for success after high school. These could be daily living skills (such as being aware of safety and preparing food, for example), social skills (such as developing confidence and responsible behavior), or occupational skills (ranging from handling a job interview to developing manual skills). All of these skills are important for all students, whether they have disabilities or not, but your job as an IEP team member is to look at your specific students and their individual needs.

By the time the student is 16, your team must look at services that will help with transition goals. To do this, the school must reach out and establish linkages with businesses and community resources. The services that might be accessed are as various as the students themselves, and they really depend on the team having a clear sense of what the student is aiming for after high school and what it will take to get there. Some services will be part of the student's high school classes and others might take place out in the community. Supervised jobs, job sampling, internships, volunteer activities, job coaching, regular or special vocational courses and programs, and specific training at community agencies might be considered by your team.

Another crucial role of the transition team is to set up service systems to support the student after he graduates. Getting access to services lined up is a major task that can take several years. Sometimes, especially when disabilities are serious, students and families will have to deal with multiple agencies to obtain services such as housing, training, health care, therapy, jobs, and funding. Different systems have different application procedures, eligibility requirements, and funding sources. Setting up services can require months of phone calls, meetings, forms and paperwork, interviews, assessments, and waiting lists.

Students and parents must be encouraged and invited by the transition team to sit down with agencies to find out what kind of support, training, and funding is available to the student. School personnel have a particular responsibility to take the lead in bringing agencies, parents, and students together. Do not assume, based on past experience, that an agency will not provide services in your particular case, since agency priorities and programs shift and change. Depending on the student, you will want to work with your state's Department of Rehabilitative Services, Department of Mental Health and Developmental Disabilities, and Department of Education. Private organizations such as the Association for Retarded Citizens and the Muscular Dystrophy Association (to name just two) can also offer services.

Meetings for and about students with severe disabilities may be intense, lengthy, and time-consuming. Parents are often very concerned about what the future will hold once the school is no longer the primary service provider. For example, what will the family do if the student is not employable? Where will this young adult live and how will he spend his days? Transportation is often a key issue outside of urban areas, where public transportation may be scarce. Even if the prospect of a job seems good, how will the young adult get to the job?

Finally, when a student reaches the age of majority, the student's IEP must include a statement that he has been informed of any rights that transfer to him upon reaching the age of majority.

The following guidelines may help your team to move through the required process of transition planning for a student who is 16. You may, of course, start this process for the student at a younger age.

Create the Climate for Transition Services:

- Provide an orientation for the IEP team members about the transition process, including its purpose and the responsibilities of each of the team members.
- Include self-determination skills as part of the student's curriculum in preparation for independent living.
- Help the parents and student to begin developing a plan for the future, looking at the areas of employment, postsecondary education, living arrangements, and community participation.
- Identify what the student will need to carry out his plan for the future.
- Identify resources, programs, and options within the school and community that could help meet the student's needs.

Before the IEP Meeting:

- Invite the parents, the student, and appropriate school and agency personnel to attend.
- Identify someone who can help the family and student as transition services are developed and carried out.
- If the student is unable to attend, take other steps to gain an understanding of the student's needs, preferences, and interests, such as completing a future plan, a functional vocational assessment, or other activities.
- Compile and review information regarding the student's needs, preferences, and interests; teacher recommendations; student and family goals; vocational assessment; and other supporting information.
- Identify and prepare information about services that might assist the student in the areas of independent living, community participation, employment, postsecondary education, and if appropriate, activities of daily living and functional vocational evaluation.

During the IEP Meeting:

- Introduce all meeting participants, including any participating agency personnel, and explain the reason for transition planning and the services, along with the roles and responsibilities of all members.
- Discuss the student's needs, preferences, and interests in the areas of post-secondary education, employment, independent living, and community participation.
- Identify long-term adult outcomes that will help the student move from high school to future education, employment, independent living, and community participation.
- Review and develop present levels of performance in the narrative of the IEP.
- Discuss and document the basis for determining that a service is not needed by the student in the areas of postsecondary education, vocational training, integrated

employment (including supported employment), continuing and adult education, adult services, independent living, or community participation.

- ▸ Identify activities and services that will support the student's long-term goals.
- ▸ Develop and record the goals and objectives that support the transition services activities identified.

After the IEP Meeting:

- ▸ Maintain communication with the student, family, teachers, and service providers to monitor the progress the student is making toward his long-term goals. Review student progress at least annually.
- ▸ If an agency fails to provide agreed upon services contained in the IEP, call for a meeting as soon as possible to identify alternative strategies to meet the transition objectives and, if necessary, revise the student's IEP.

Chapter 13
What Happens When People Don't Agree

As in any other area of life, disagreements sometimes pop up among IEP team members about the educational program for a student with a disability. For example, perhaps you, as a general education teacher, feel that a "pull out" program would be the most appropriate and least restrictive environment for providing supplementary instruction in reading for a student with a learning disability. But perhaps the parents disagree and insist that this service should be provided in the general education classroom. Your team is stuck and can't seem to agree on what is best for the student. So what happens now?

The best way to resolve conflicts is usually informally. It is quicker, and less adversarial if you can find a way for your team to move forward without having to engage in more formal proceedings. This is particularly true if your team has to go to due process proceedings, which will involve considerable cost, time, energy, and thought on the part of the school and the parents. Perhaps you can find someone who can sit with your group and help you find a way past the impasse. This person should be a good listener and mediator and someone who everybody trusts to help. Try to stay open minded if you are involved in a dispute of this sort, as conflicts are hard to solve when people take entrenched positions. Remind everyone that when all the dust settles, the school and the family still have to work together.

But informal problem-solving does not always work, and IDEA is quite specific about the rights of schools and parents, as well as the procedures that must be followed when people disagree. This chapter will begin to introduce you to those requirements, but you should contact your local special education director if you are having problems of this kind. State and local procedures will spell out exactly what your team must do if they cannot agree.

IDEA describes both "mediation" and "due process" procedures for resolving disputes between parents and schools. These terms will be described in this chapter. Parents should also know that they can file a complaint directly to the state department of education, which is sometimes simpler than engaging in mediation or due process. But the choice lies with the parents.

Mediation and due process only apply to disputes about the *legal* obligations of states and schools to students with disabilities. At the most basic level, for example, states must provide students with disabilities with a free appropriate public education in the least restrictive environment. Parents have the right to dissent about any matter relating to the identification, evaluation, or placement of their student. These matters involve the school's legal obligation to the student, and mediation and due process regulations apply.

But maybe the dispute does not concern the legal obligations of the state. This may happen when the difficulties are personal or the school is following state and local regulations in accomplishing certain tasks, but the parents find the process slow or cumbersome. If you are involved in a dispute, contact your local special education director to find out if the disagreement is about a legal obligation of the school.

Your school district has certain obligations called "procedural safeguards" to make sure that parents are informed about certain aspects or changes in the student's program. For example, parents must be notified when the school wants to change or refuses to change a student's identification, evaluation, or educational placement. Parents must also be informed of their rights to such items as an independent evaluation of the student, their access to educational records, mediation, due process, and appeals. These must be written in a clearly understandable way and in the parent's native language, unless it is clearly not feasible to do so.

- New in 1997: Parental consent must be obtained before the school conducts any reevaluation of a student with disabilities. This is true unless the school can demonstrate that it has taken reasonable steps to obtain the consent, but the parent did not respond.

Previously, states have established broad guidelines for mediations to resolve disputes between parents and schools. But as of 1997, each state must establish a voluntary mediation system and cover its costs. Mediation is meant to be an "intermediary step" between informal problem-solving and the more formal due process procedure. Now, parents must be offered mediation whenever a due process hearing is requested.

What are the new requirements regarding mediation procedures? Mediation procedures must meet the following requirements:

- Mediation must be voluntary. It is not required.
- The procedure must be conducted by a qualified and impartial mediator who is trained in effective mediation techniques.
- Mediation is free to its participants. The state pays the cost.
- Each mediation session must be scheduled in a timely manner and held in a location that is convenient to the disputing parties.
- Any agreement reached during the mediation process must be described in a written mediation agreement.
- Discussions that occur during the mediation process must be confidential and may not be used as evidence in any subsequent due process hearings or civil proceedings. The parties to the mediation process may be required to sign a confidentiality pledge before the mediation process.

▸ A school district may require that parents who don't choose mediation must meet with a disinterested party who would explain the benefits of mediation and encourage the parents to use it. This meeting must be held at a time and location that is convenient to the parents. But the school district may not deny or delay a parent's right to a due process hearing if the parent fails to participate in this meeting.

States must keep a list of qualified mediators who are knowledgeable about the laws and regulations for special education. Whenever a mediator is not selected randomly from this list, then the parents and the school should work together and agree on who the mediator will be.

Whether parents choose mediation or not, they are always entitled to due process proceedings if they have complaints about the identification, evaluation, or educational placement of their student, or if they think that a free and appropriate education has not been provided for the student. The due process procedure is more formal than mediation, and it has its own regulations. The process starts when a parent or the parent's attorney writes to the state or local education agency with a complaint, a description of the problem, and a proposed resolution. Each state education agency has a form that the parents or attorneys can use to file a complaint.

In 1997, a new provision was added to the due process procedure. At least 5 days before the hearing, both the school and the parents must show one another any evaluations and recommendations that they intend to use during the hearing. If either party does not disclose this information, they may not be able to use it during the due process hearing.

The due process hearing is conducted by a qualified and impartial person who is not employed by a public agency that is involved in the student's education or care. Each state has a list of people who are qualified to serve as hearing officers. The exact procedure of the hearing is described by state and local laws.

Any party to a due process hearing or appeal has the right to

▸ Be accompanied and advised by an attorney or lay advocate, and by people who have special knowledge or training with respect to the problems of students with disabilities.
▸ Present evidence, confront and cross-examine witnesses, and compel the attendance of witnesses.
▸ Prohibit the introduction of any evidence at the hearing that has not been disclosed to that party at least 5 days before the hearing.
▸ Obtain a written (or, at the option of the parents, taped) verbatim record of the hearing.
▸ Obtain written (or, at the option of the parents, taped) copy of the hearing's findings and decisions.

Parents involved in hearings also have the right to

- ▸ Have the student who is the subject of the hearing present.
- ▸ Open the hearing to the public.
- ▸ Receive the "reasonable" cost of attorney's fees, under certain specific circumstances, if the hearing officer rules in the parent's favor.

The local school district is required to ensure that within 45 days after receiving a parent's request for a hearing

- ▸ The hearing officer reaches a final decision about the case.
- ▸ A copy of the decision is sent to the parents and to the school.

The decision made in the due process hearing is final, unless one of the parties files an appeal and asks for a hearing from the state board of education. Then, someone at the state level will review the case, gather additional information if necessary, and make a decision within 30 days. If either party is still dissatisfied, it can file suit with a state or federal district court. This is a lengthy process in which the court reviews the case, hears additional evidence if requested, makes a decision, and directs the losing party to remedy the problem.

What happens to a student with disabilities while a dispute about his program is going on? The student would remain in his current educational program, unless the parents and school system agree on another program. Also, if the student is applying to attend a public school while the dispute is going on, the student would be admitted to the school (with the parent's consent) until the dispute has been resolved.

If you are involved in a dispute with parents over a student's educational program, then you need to think about the evidence that support your position and weigh it against any evidence that the parents may have. What written evaluations, assessments, exam results, observations or checklists supports your position? What are your qualifications to make the judgment, and what are the qualifications of any people who would support your view? The school district is the party with standing and should work with you to prepare for hearings and court appearances.

Resolving differences within the due process system is not a decision to be made lightly. Try, before your team's disagreements get to this point, to get help to consider all points of view, and try mediation if the parents will agree. If the matter reaches all the way to the courts, a resolution will come far too late to serve any immediate needs that a student with disabilities may have.

Appendix I
Definitions of Legal Terms Contained Within IDEA '97

ASSISTIVE TECHNOLOGY DEVICE means any item, piece of equipment, or product system, whether acquired commercially off the shelf, modified, or customized, that is used to increase, maintain, or improve the functional capabilities of a student with a disability.

ASSISTIVE TECHNOLOGY SERVICE means any service that directly assists a student with a disability in the selection, acquisition, or use of an assistive technology device, including

- The evaluation of the student's needs, including a functional evaluation of the student in his customary environment.
- Purchasing, leasing, or otherwise providing for the acquisition of assistive technology devices by the student.
- Selecting, designing, fitting, customizing, adapting, applying, maintaining, repairing, or replacing of assistive technology devices.
- Coordinating and using other therapies, interventions, or services with assistive technology devices, such as those associated with existing education and rehabilitation plans and programs.
- Training or technical assistance for the student, or, where appropriate, the family of the student.
- Training or technical assistance for professionals (including individuals providing education and rehabilitation services), employers, or other individuals who provide services to, employ, or are otherwise substantially involved in the major life functions of the student.

EARLY INTERVENTION SERVICES means developmental services that

- Are provided under public supervision.
- Are provided at no cost except where federal or state law provides for a system of payments by families, including a schedule of sliding fees.
- Are designed to meet the developmental needs of an infant or toddler with a disability in any one or more of the following areas: physical, cognitive, communication, social or emotional development, or adaptive development.
- Meet federal and state standards.

- Include family training, counseling, and home visits; special instruction; speech-language pathology and audiology services; occupational therapy; physical therapy; psychological services; service coordination services; medical services only for diagnostic or evaluation purposes; early identification, screening, and assessment services; health services necessary to enable the infant or toddler to benefit from the other early intervention services; social work services; vision services; assistive technology devices and assistive technology services; and transportation and related costs that are necessary to enable an infant or toddler and the infant's or toddler's family to receive another service described in this paragraph.
- Are provided by qualified personnel, including special educators, speech-language pathologists and audiologists, occupational therapists, physical therapists, psychologists, social workers, nurses, nutritionists, family therapists, orientation and mobility specialists, and pediatricians and other physicians.
- To the maximum extent appropriate, are provided in natural environments, including the home, and community settings in which children without disabilities participate.
- Are provided in conformity with an individualized family service plan adopted in accordance with federal requirements.

FREE APPROPRIATE PUBLIC EDUCATION means special education and related services that

- Have been provided at public expense, under public supervision and direction, and without charge.
- Meet the standards of the state educational agency.
- Include an appropriate preschool, elementary, or secondary school education in the state involved.
- Are provided in conformity with the individualized education program.

INDIVIDUALIZED EDUCATION PROGRAM OR IEP means a written statement for each student with a disability that is developed, reviewed, and revised in accordance with IDEA's requirements.

INDIVIDUALIZED FAMILY SERVICE PLAN (or IFSP) is a written plan developed by a multidisciplinary team, including the parents, that contains

- A statement of the infant's or toddler's present levels of physical, cognitive, communication, developmental, social or emotional, and adaptive development, based on objective criteria.
- A statement of the family's resources, priorities, and concerns relating to enhancing the development of the family's infant or toddler with a disability.
- A statement of the major outcomes expected to be achieved for the infant or toddler and the family, and the criteria, procedures, and timelines used to

determine the degree to which progress toward achieving the outcomes is being made and whether modifications or revisions of the outcomes or services are necessary.

- A statement of specific early intervention services necessary to meet the unique needs of the infant or toddler and the family, including the frequency, intensity, and method of delivering services.
- A statement of the natural environments in which early intervention services shall appropriately be provided, including a justification of the extent, if any, to which the services will not be provided in a natural environment.
- The projected dates for initiation of services and the anticipated duration of the services.
- The identification of the service coordinator from the profession most immediately relevant to the infant's or toddler's or family's needs (or who is otherwise qualified to carry out all applicable responsibilities) who will be responsible for the implementation of the plan and coordination with other agencies and persons.
- The steps to be taken to support the transition of the toddler with a disability to preschool or other appropriate services.

INFANT OR TODDLER WITH A DISABILITY means a child under 3 years of age who needs early intervention services because he

- Is experiencing developmental delays, as measured by appropriate diagnostic instruments and procedures in one or more of the areas of cognitive, physical, communication, social or emotional, and adaptive development; or
- Has a diagnosed physical or mental condition which has a high probability of resulting in developmental delay.

This term may also include, at a state's discretion, at-risk infants and toddlers.

NATIVE LANGUAGE. The term "native language," when used with reference to an individual of limited English proficiency, means the language normally used by the individual, or in the case of a student, the language normally used by the student's parents.

RELATED SERVICES means transportation, and such developmental, corrective, and other supportive services (including speech-language pathology and audiology services; psychological services; physical and occupational therapy; recreation, including therapeutic recreation; social work services; counseling services, including rehabilitation counseling; orientation and mobility services; and medical services, except that such medical services shall be for diagnostic and evaluation purposes only) as may be required to assist a student with a disability to benefit from special education, and includes the early identification and assessment of disabling conditions in children.

SPECIAL EDUCATION means specially designed instruction, at no cost to parents, to meet the unique needs of a student with a disability, including

- Instruction conducted in the classroom, in the home, in hospitals and institutions, and in other settings.
- Instruction in physical education.

SPECIFIC LEARNING DISABILITY means a disorder in one or more of the basic psychological processes involved in understanding or in using language, spoken or written, which may be manifested in an imperfect ability to listen, think, speak, read, write, spell, or do mathematical calculations. This term includes such conditions as perceptual disabilities, brain injury, minimal brain dysfunction, dyslexia, and developmental aphasia. This term does not include a learning problem that is primarily the result of visual, hearing, or motor disabilities; of mental retardation; of emotional disturbance; or of environmental, cultural, or economic disadvantage.

STUDENT WITH A DISABILITY means

- A student with mental retardation, hearing impairments (including deafness), speech or language impairments, visual impairments (including blindness), serious emotional disturbance, orthopedic impairments, autism, traumatic brain injury, other health impairments, or specific learning disabilities; and
- Who, because of these disabilities, needs special education and related services.

The term "student with a disability" for a student aged 3 through 9 may, at the discretion of the state and the local educational agency, include

- A child who is experiencing developmental delays, as defined by the state and as measured by appropriate diagnostic instruments and procedures, in one or more of the following areas: physical, cognitive, communication, social or emotional, or adaptive development; and
- Who, because of these difficulties, need special education and related services.

SUPPLEMENTARY AIDS AND SERVICES means, aids, services, and other supports that are provided in general education classes or other education-related settings to enable students with disabilities to be educated with nondisabled students to the maximum extent appropriate.

TRANSITION SERVICES means a coordinated set of activities for a student with a disability that

- Is designed within an outcome-oriented process, which promotes movement from school to postschool activities, including postsecondary education, vocational training, integrated employment (including supported employment), continuing and adult education, adult services, independent living, or community participation.

- ▸ Is based upon the individual student's needs, taking into account the student's preferences and interests.
- ▸ Includes instruction, related services, community experiences, the development of employment and other postschool adult living objectives, and, when appropriate, acquisition of daily living skills and functional vocational evaluation.

Appendix II
Sources for More Information

Chapter 1:   IDEA '97: Revisioning Special and General Education as One System

The Center for Policy Research on the Impact of General and Special Education Reform. (1998). *The push and pull of standards-based reform: how does it affect local school districts and students with disabilities?* Alexandria, VA: National Association of State Boards of Education.

The Center for Policy Research on the Impact of General and Special Education Reform. (1996). *What will it take? Standards-based education reform for all students.* Alexandria, VA: National Association of State Boards of Education.

McDonnell, L. M., McLaughlin, M., & Patricia Morison. (Eds. 1997). *Educating one and all: Students with disabilities and standards-based reform.* Washington, DC: National Academy Press.

Chapter 3:   The IEP Team Members

Field, S., Martin, J., Miller, R., Ward, M., & Wehmeyer, M. (1998). *A practical guide for teaching self-determination.* Reston, VA: The Council for Exceptional Children.

Field, S. & Hoffman, A. (1996). *Steps to self-determination: A curriculum to help adolescents learn to achieve their goals.* Arlington, TX: Pro-Ed.

Sitlington, P., Neubert, D., Begun, W., Lombard, R., & Leconte, P. (1996). *Assess for success: Handbook on transition assessment.* Reston, VA: The Council for Exceptional Children.

Wehmeyer, M. & Kelchner, K. (1995). *The Arc's self-determination scale: Adolescent version.* Arlington, TX: The Arc of the United States.

Chapter 4:   The IEP Team as a Team

Brolin, D. (1997). *Life centered career education: A competency based approach, fifth edition.* Reston, VA: The Council for Exceptional Children.

Friend, M. & Cook, L. (1996). *Interactions: Collaboration skills for school professionals, second edition*. White Plains, NY: Longman Publishers.

Wehmeyer, M. & Kelchner, K. (1995). *The Arc's self-determination scale: Adolescent version*. Arlington, TX: The Arc of the United States.

Chapter 6:   Assessing the Present Level of Educational Performance and Developing Measurable Goals, Short-Term Objectives, and Benchmarks

Poulson, J. & Fognani-Smaus, K. (1997). Using the IEP as a tool to access curriculum and instruction. Aurora, CO: Aurora Public Schools.

Chapter 10:   Special Factors (Behavior, Diversity, Braille, Communication Needs, and Assistive Technology), Physical Education, and the Extended School Year

Center for Effective Collaboration and Practice. (1998). *Addressing student problem behavior: An IEP team's introduction to functional behavior assessment and behavior intervention plans*. Washington, DC: American Institutes for Research.

Council of Administrators of Special Education Division of The Council for Exceptional Children (1997). *Has technology been considered? A guide for IEP teams*. Albuquerque, NM: The Council of Administrators of Special Education and the Technology and Media Division of The Council for Exceptional Children.

Chapter 12:   The Transition to Adult Life

Sitlington, P., Neubert, D. Begun, W., Lombard, R., & Leconte, P. (1996). *Assess for success: Handbook on transition assessment*. Reston, VA: The Council for Exceptional Children.

West, L., Corbey, S., Arden, B., Jones, B., Miller, R., & Sarkees-Wircenski, M. (1992). *Integrating transition planning into the IEP process*. Reston, VA: The Council for Exceptional Children.

Appendix III
Bibliography

Anderson, W., Chitwood, S., & Hayden, D. (1997). *Negotiating the special education maze: A guide for parents and teachers.* Bethesda, MD: Woodbine House.

Asselin, S., Todd-Allen, M, & deFur, S. (1998). Transition coordinators: Define yourselves. Reston, VA: *TEACHING Exceptional Children, 30* (3).

Aurora Public Schools. (1997). *Guide to completion of the individual education plan.* Aurora, CO: Aurora Public Schools.

Cahir, W. J. (1997, July 17). 1997 Individuals with Disabilities Education Act analysis. *Education Daily Special Supplement, 30,* (137).

The Center for Policy Research on the Impact of General and Special Education Reform. (1998). *The push and pull of standards-based reform: How does it affect local school districts and students with disabilities?* Alexandria, VA: National Association of State Boards of Education.

The Council for Exceptional Children. (1998). *IDEA reauthorization: Focus on the IEP and assessment.* Reston, VA: Taped Telecast by The Council for Exceptional Children.

The Council for Exceptional Children. (1998). *IDEA 1997: Let's make it work.* Reston, VA: The Council for Exceptional Children.

The Council for Exceptional Children. (1997). A winning combination: LCCE, the student-led IEP, and self determination. Reston, VA: *The LCCE Insider, 1* (2) 1 and 7.

Elliot, J. L., Erickson, R. N., Thurlow, M. L., & Shriner, J. (in press). State-level accountability for the performance of students with disabilities: Five years of change? *Journal of Special Education.*

Friend, M. & Cook, L. (1996). *Interactions: Collaboration skills for school professionals, second edition.* White Plains, NY: Longman Publishers.

Gandal, M. (1997). *Making standards matter: An annual fifty-state report on efforts to raise academic standards.* Washington, DC: American Federation of Teachers, Educational Issues Department.

Individuals with Disabilities Education Act Amendments of 1997 (IDEA, as amended), P.L. 105-17. (June 4, 1997). Title 20, U.S.C. 1400 et seq; Congressional Record, Volume 140 (1994).

Individuals with Disabilities Education Act Amendments of 1997, *Senate Report* 105-17.

Martin, J. E., & Marshall, L. H. (1995). ChoiceMaker: A comprehensive self-determination transition program. *Intervention in School and Clinic, 30,* 147-156.

McIntire, J. (1997a). *Implications with the changes brought about in the IDEA reauthorization related to the development and implementation of an individualized education program (IEP).* Unpublished paper prepared for The Council for Exceptional Children.

McIntire, J. (1997b). *The individualized education program: An evolving document for parents and educators.* Unpublished paper prepared for The Council for Exceptional Children.

The National Commission on Excellence in Education (1983). A nation at risk: The imperative for educational reform. Washington, DC: U.S. Government Printing Office.

Ohio Department of Education, Division of Special Education and Division of Early Childhood Education (1995). *The individualized education program (IEP): A tour book for the journey.* Worthington, OH: Ohio Department of Education.

Poulson, J. & Fognani-Smaus, K. (1997). *Using the IEP as a tool to access curriculum and instruction.* Aurora, CO: Aurora Public Schools.

Smith, M., & O'Day, J. (1993). Systemic reform and educational opportunity, in S. Fuhrman, (Ed.), *Designing coherent policy: Improving the system.* San Francisco, CA: Jossey-Bass.

Smith, M., & O'Day, J. (1990). Systemic School Reform. *Politics of Education Association Yearbook 1990,* 223-267.

Thurlow M. L., Langenfeld, K., Nelson, R., Shin, H., & Coleman, J. (1997). *State accountability reports: What do they say about students with disabilities?* (Technical Report 20). Minneapolis, MN: University of Minnesota, National Center on Educational Outcomes.

U.S. Department of Education (1997). Assistance to states for the education of children with disabilities, preschool grants for children with disabilities, and early intervention program for infants and toddlers with disabilities; proposed rule. *Federal Register, 62*, (204), 55025-55135. Microfiche.

West, L., Corbey, S., Arden, B., Jones, B., Miller, R., & Sarkees-Wircenski, M. (1992). *Integrating transition planning into the IEP process.* Reston, VA: The Council for Exceptional Children.

Vaughn, S., Schumm, J. S., & Arguelles, M. E. (1997). The ABCDEs of co-teaching, *TEACHING Exceptional Children, 30* (2), 4-10.